THE ESSENTIAL LANDSCAPE

Joan Myers, *San Miguel, New Mexico*

The Essential Landscape

The New Mexico Photographic Survey
with essays by J.B. Jackson

Steven A. Yates, Editor
Photographers: Thomas F. Barrow, Miguel Gandert, Alex Harris,
Paul Logsdon, Joan Myers, Anne Noggle, Mary Peck,
Bernard Plossu, Edward Ranney, Meridel Rubenstein,
Richard Wickstrom, Richard Wilder

The University of New Mexico Press
Albuquerque

Library of Congress Cataloging in Publication Data
Main entry under title:

The essential landscape.

   Photographic project of the Museum of Fine Arts, Museum of
New Mexico.
   1. New Mexico—Description and travel—1981–   —Addresses,
essays, lectures. 2. New Mexico—Description and travel—1981–
   —Views. 3. Landscape assessment—New Mexico—Addresses,
essays, lectures. 4. Photography, Artistic. I. Yates, Steve. II. Barrow,
Thomas F. III. Jackson, John Brinckerhoff, 1909–   . IV. Museum of
New Mexico. Museum of Fine Arts. V. Title: New Mexico
Photographic Survey.
F796.5.E85   1985   779'.99789   84-23754
ISBN 0-8263-0784-1

"The Social Landscape" reprinted by permission of the University of
Massachusetts Press.

The seven essays that originally appeared in *Landscape* reprinted by
permission.

Contents

Preface

Not since the establishment of the Santa Fe Trail in the last century has New Mexico undergone such a significant period of growth. The New Mexico Photographic Survey began in response to this time of transformation and decisive change. Created under the auspices of the Museum of New Mexico, the Survey provided the working context in which twelve photographers living in New Mexico could rediscover the state and gave them the opportunity to create bodies of work that reflect its unique qualities. The project was designed to encourage and sustain each photographer's individual method of working and to allow ideas to develop over several years. Their responses are translated through personal styles and vision, which augment the documentary value of their photographs.

Thus, what is depicted is the result of human bias. The Survey displays insights from individual points of view and personal experiences that magnify the nature of this landscape. The sense of individual experience and the photographer's intuition are influential supplements to the value of the subject itself. What we discover in this work is not eclipsed by self-expression or technical exercise. Yet, to disregard either aspect in the shaping of these photographers' ideas is to deny their full dimensions.

The selection of essays by J. B. Jackson complements the photographic works by articulating the underlying nature of this complex human landscape. As a highly perceptive observer and cultural geographer of American landscapes, Jackson writes about the vernacular character of this land. Like the photographers, he rejects popular notions and clichés in seeking a deeper understanding through uncommon vision. The traces of human presence in the landscape provide him with a provocative vocabulary of our time. These essays and photographs all provide refined expressions of the experience of seeing New Mexico.

The Photographic Survey represents the expressive potentials of photography but mirrors no single school of thought. It reflects the vitality and diversity as well as the many philosophies in American photography today. These essays and works help establish a picture of contemporary New Mexico, although our rich cultural identity demands continued questioning in this era of significant change. What J. B. Jackson and these twelve photographers present is a contemporary frame of reference in the essence and evolution of this land.

Steve Yates
Curator of Photography
Museum of New Mexico

*The depth of human experience . . . depends on the
fact that we are able to vary our modes of seeing, that
we can alternate our views of reality.*

*Art gives us a richer, more vivid and colorful image of
reality, and a more profound insight into its formal
structure. It is characteristic of the nature of man that
he is not limited to one specific approach to reality,
but can choose his point of view.*

—Ernst Cassirer

*. . . art is by nature an origin: a distinctive way in
which truth comes into being. . . .*

—Martin Heidegger

THE ESSENTIAL LANDSCAPE

Looking at New Mexico

We learn about history by reading it in school; we learn to see it when we travel, and for Americans the place where we see most clearly the impact of time on a landscape is New Mexico.

Our history is more complicated than most, and it is far more visible. In regions to the east of us, more prosperous and blessed with more abundant rainfall, the past, even the recent past, soon vanishes from sight: bulldozed out of existence in favor of something new and larger and more costly, it is also often quickly hidden by exuberant vegetation. Even the rubble of abandoned tenements in the Bronx soon acquires a covering of weeds and vines, and sometimes wildflowers; trees conceal the abandoned farms of Appalachia. But here in New Mexico history remains exposed to the sun for all to see. Our landscape is everywhere spotted with ruins—ruins of ancient towns, ruins of sheepherders' shelters built a decade ago. It is as if we had been struck by a neutron bomb eliminating people while leaving their dwellings intact, at the mercy of wind and sun. It is to see our past that thousands of tourists come to New Mexico: archeologists, geologists,

antiquarians, lovers of whatever is old or out-of-date or mysterious because of its age. Our history invites the photographer.

The best time for seeing history is the summer. That is when the remoter country can be explored; it is when schools and colleges all over America are closed, and teachers and students and scholars are free to wander. It follows, therefore, that awareness of southwestern history is a seasonal phenomenon determined by the academic calendar, much as a certain kind of piety is determined by phases of the moon. Summer is the time for looking back and recording what we see. Family reunions, two hundred strong, gather in the shade of a cottonwood grove, in a dance hall, in a half-forgotten village once an ancestral stronghold. Veterans' organizations parade down Main Street, and Santa Fe and Wagon Mound and Arroyo Seco deck themselves out in Indian or Spanish-American or cowboy or counterculture costume, celebrating the Old Days. The sun shines out of a deep blue sky; it is hot, but not too hot, and history is transformed into a photographic pageant, an ideal subject for color slides.

Yet it is hard not to be fleetingly aware of a background

suggestive of a kind of history with a different dimension, no matter where we are in New Mexico. We glimpse it in a dark face in the crowd; we catch an echo of it in the voices and the music coming from a corner bar. We see and never quite forget the horizon of range after range of mountains of diminishing blue. In every background there lurks another kind of past, far more ancient, far less easy to comprehend than the strictly human history on display.

There is one region of New Mexico where we can come closer to a time measured not by events or seasons but by millennia, a landscape with a history of its own that is perhaps not history at all, merely the unending repetition of cosmic cycles, a landscape where by a paradox the still photograph records all we can ever know of its past. The Colorado Plateau is the name given by geographers and geologists to an immense region covering most of Utah, western Colorado, eastern Arizona, and northwestern New Mexico. When you drive due west of Albuquerque toward Grants and the uranium country, you catch a glimpse of a small portion of it—a horizon like a long, pale blue rampart, extending beyond sight to the north and south. It is deceptively unspectacular, almost a continuation, one would say, of the pleasantly humanized landscape of the Rio Grande country. But this is actually only the eastern edge of a province distinguished by its great elevation (reaching in places to 11,000 feet), its hundreds of remarkable canyons (including the Grand Canyon), and its overall horizontality. Every mesa, every canyon, every free-standing mountain seems composed of layer upon layer of red and brown and yellow and dead white rock. Only a small fragment of this spectacular landscape lies in New Mexico, but it is a fragment containing some of the largest prehistoric ruins in the United States, as well as areas with occasional stands of trees and small streams meandering through canyons. There are expanses of pale grass and sagebrush, and piñon

and juniper trees in groves on the slopes of the valleys. It seems to be empty of life, but in summer it sometimes has a strangely pastoral, almost arcadian quality. Navajos graze their flocks of goats and sheep on the grass among the miniature forests of sagebrush, bells tinkling. In the middle of the day they rest in the dense black shade of the piñons. The air is fragrant, the light on the perpendicular dark red canyon walls is golden. Small clusters of ragged Navajo dwellings, with a peach tree or two nearby, stand under the piñon trees, and a saddle horse sleepily hangs his head. Turn elsewhere and the view is perhaps a little too vast for comfort: a panorama of endless range country with a rim of violet mesas and dark mountains where there must be forests and streams of water, though very far away. The days are all alike; the summer is long and immobile. In the late afternoon immense black clouds boil up to the zenith, and then some small portion of the hot and thirsty landscape is suddenly blessed with a brief, violent downpour which makes every rock, every patch of earth glisten. The storm comes to an abrupt end like a duty routinely performed, and is followed by not one but two perfect rainbows. It is as if some rite had been reenacted, some myth made visible for the millionth time, antiphony to a ceremonial dance in a nearby Indian village.

Which comes first: the blessing or the prayer? It is not easy in this landscape to separate the role of man from the role of nature. The plateau country has been lived in for centuries, but the human presence is disguised even from the camera's eye. There are ruins like geological formations, disorders of tumbled stone. There are immense arrays of slowly crumbling rocks that look like ruins. The nomenclature we Americans have imposed on much of the landscape testifies to our uncertainty: the ruins have unpronounceable Navajo names; the natural formations are called Gothic Mesa or Monument Valley or Chimney Rock.

2

It is the sort of landscape which (before the creation of the bomb) we associated with the world after history had come to an end: sheep grazing among long-abandoned ruins, the lesson of Ozymandias driven home by enormous red arches leading nowhere, lofty red obelisks or needles commemorating events no one had ever heard of, symbols of the vanity of human endeavor waiting to be photographed. But is that really the message of the plateau country? There was a time, several generations ago, toward the end of the last century when photographers, masters of their art, had a clearer vision: they wanted to leave history, even human beings, out of their pictures. Perhaps there were technical reasons for wishing to exclude all movement, or perhaps it was a matter of belief, a way of responding to the concept of time in the Colorado Plateau. For what makes the landscape so impressive and so beautiful is that it teaches no copybook moral, no ecological or social lesson. It tells us that there is another way of measuring time, and that the present is, in fact, an enormous interval in which even the newest of man-made structures are contemporary with the primaeval. That is why it is possible to see that the dams on the Colorado and San Juan rivers, the deep pits of the Santa Rita copper mines, and the terraced mountains near Laguna where uranium has been extracted are all as old or as young as the canyons and mesas and the undulating plains of sagebrush. Not far from Quemado (which is not far from the Arizona line) there is a field of innumerable lightning rods, geometrically planted in an expanse of range grass. As an example of contemporary environmental art it is a source of infinite curiosity and bewilderment. Some day, centuries hence, the field of lightning rods will have been forgotten by tourists and entirely assimilated into the landscape. Navajos grazing their sheep among them will know that these rods derive from the same cosmic occurrence that balanced liver-colored rocks

on pedestals of yellow mud in the Chaco region: objects identified with an Emergence myth, easily explained, provided our small-scale micro-history is left out of the picture.

II

That school of "timeless" photography flourished at a period when all of New Mexico was described by outsiders, and even admiringly described, in terms of its peculiar notions of time. It was "the land of poco-tiempo," "the land of mañana," "the land where time stood still." What was meant was not Indian or prehistoric New Mexico, but Spanish-American New Mexico.

By and large this is the New Mexico associated with the upper Rio Grande Valley and the mountains containing it. For it was here that the first colonists settled in the late sixteenth century, and it was here that the province (or state) acquired its identity. What attracted settlement was the mild climate, the apparent abundance of water, the fertile soil, and the forests covering the mountains. In many ways the landscape seemed to resemble that of Spain. Almost from the time of the first explorations New Mexico was seen as a kind of promised land: not a paradise of ease and abundance, to be sure, but a land of grass and forests and flowing water where the efforts of working men and women would be duly rewarded. For it so happens, even today, that no matter whether you come to New Mexico from the immediate east, the High Plains, the arid south, or the canyon landscape in the west, the region always seems, by comparison with the country you have been traveling through, something like a land flowing with milk and honey. What shatters the illusion is the long, dry summer that afflicts the greater part of the state.

How long it took the earlier generations of Spanish-speaking colonists to learn that lesson is a complicated question: the presence of hostile Indians in the plains of the eastern part of New Mexico acted to discourage their settlement and even exploration until the mid-eighteenth century. In any event, Spanish settlement was long confined to the Rio Grande region, which to this day remains the heartland of Spanish-American culture. The small lateral valleys of the Rio Grande, as well as the valley of the Rio Grande itself, provided the colonists with an environment suited to their kind of agriculture and their kind of living—in small villages where old established customs and relationships could be continued. Settlement in colonial New Mexico was in effect a transplantation, a new version of the order that had prevailed in colonial Mexico and in Spain. It was not the work of footloose individuals in search of adventures or wealth, but of small, homogeneous groups of simple people who brought with them their religion, their family ties, their ways of building and working and farming.

Farming meant irrigation; to that extent they were aware of the climatic limitations of the region, and they knew that the only places where that kind of farming was possible were along the few permanent water courses in the foothills and valleys. Each village devised its own communal irrigation system—an accomplishment deserving of more recognition than it has so far received; and each village gradually created its own miniature landscape of gardens and orchards and fields and pastures, a landscape distinct from the surrounding wilderness. Farmers not only introduced new kinds of vegetation—crops and grasses and fruit trees—but also another climate, for their irrigation system made them relatively independent of the unpredictable local rains.

The history of these villages is largely unrecorded; all we usually know about them is roughly the decade of their settlement, the date of the first church, and place of origin of its first settlers. Indian raids, feuds with neighboring villages, the building of a road to the outside world—important events in their time—remain a matter of legend or hearsay. The destruction of the irrigation system by a cloudburst, the erosion of fields, the gradual destruction of the nearby forest, and the gradual desertion of the village itself—these are confirmed by visual evidence. But what is lacking is any picture of the villages in their prime. Those of us who are old enough can remember places in the foothills of the Sangre de Cristos or in the valleys of the Rio Puerco, the Pecos, the Rio Grande as they were a half century ago. They had already begun to decline, and signs of increasing poverty and depopulation were painfully clear, yet there were still cultivated fields and well-kept irrigation ditches; there was a general store, there was a school, there was a freshly painted church and a neat graveyard. On Sunday afternoons the young men of the village and from the nearby ranches, dressed in finery, galloped up and down the only street. There were still men and women in those days who could identify the village which a stranger came from by his accent, who knew the local name for every field, every hill, every wild plant. They knew their landscape by heart.

One after another, over the decades, they died, but like all other small farm villages, not without a struggle. A flood buried gardens and fields under gravel or sand; a local resource—wood or game or a special crop—lost its market; a railroad ceased operation; the school was closed. Rather than abandon their home, the villagers became ranchers and raised cattle or sheep. But in the end it died, and others died: first the remote villages on the margin of the plains, where there were no other jobs, and then the villages where the rangeland had deteriorated and the cedars and junipers were coming back into the abandoned fields. Now all that is left of that traditional farming landscape are the villages in the mountain heartland and in the Rio Grande Valley.

Time in those secluded places has a special flavor—a resigned, slow, autumnal beat. The colors linger into the early winter, in the brown and orange leaves on the cottonwoods along the streams and irrigation ditches, in the strings of red chili on the fronts of houses, and in the groves of lemon-yellow aspens far up in the mountains. Then a winter wind sends all their leaves to the ground in a shower of gold, and the chamisa turns grey.

Snow that lasts comes in later November and remains on the higher slopes of the Sangre de Cristos and the Jemez until well into the spring. In the valley and in the foothills it slowly melts, leaving patches hiding under the piñon trees, but in the heights and in places the sun reaches only for a few hours a day, winter is a season to be taken seriously. It transforms the smaller dirt roads into lanes of bottomless mud. The rancher stays close to headquarters, and villagers think twice before driving their mud-splattered pickups into the forest after firewood; even in town we are careful to stay on the paved surfaces. What was recently a landscape of coming and going and outdoor work—a landscape of gardens and orchards and small farms—almost overnight has turned into a scattering of isolated villages and hamlets. The cold and the wretched roads make every community, every family shrink into itself, and the silence is rarely broken. In the old days the clanking of tire chains was part of winter in the country, but in the mountains of northern New Mexico, as elsewhere, we no longer hear it, and the almost perfect soundlessness is what visitors notice first of all. Find out for yourself what this means: stand on a hillside overlooking a village of tin-roofed houses on the edge of the forest in the Sangre de Cristos or in some part of the Pecos Valley;

if it is a bright day in January or February you will hear the screaming of flickers in the groves of piñon. Then in a backyard, perhaps a half mile away, someone is slowly chopping wood. Go down into the village where there are the familiar sounds of melting snow coming off the tin roofs or out of the canales. Not a voice is heard; life has withdrawn into the houses behind closed doors, and the windows, with their displays of geraniums in tin cans, are half obscured by frost. Someone tries to start a car but soon gives up. In the cold, starry night the lights are few and dim, and you can barely make out the landscape of black forest and small, snow-covered fields. If you are lucky you may hear, very late at night, the yelp of a coyote. It sets the village dogs into a brief frenzy of barking.

It is hard to remember, despite all we have read about the history of this landscape, that as the crow flies (or as the car travels), Mexico, once the motherland, is not distant. But it is separated from us by more than barriers of mountains and desert. Snow and total darkness have imposed a kind of environmental Calvinism on northern New Mexico that all but obliterates the historic ties with that talkative and gregarious nation south of the Rio Grande, and not even the happiness of summer can entirely dispel it. Climate, no less than an ingrained sense of what is fitting, clears the plazas and the lanes of the last summer idlers, one leg propped against the wall, talking in grave voices. Climate, coupled with loyalty to family, keeps us home where we sit in silence, pondering old grievances and searching our souls. Outside, the clear bright air smells of snow and piñon smoke; inside it smells of coffee and roasting chili and wet clothes drying near the stove. Climate, sooner or later, makes us return to origins, makes the tourists and environmentalists and students of folklore and handicrafts scurry back to Berkeley or New York or Dallas to show their brightly colored slides of the Land of Enchantment, and to dream of owning an adobe house of their own, with hollyhocks in the front yard, and a loom or a potter's wheel or a dulcimer in the cool, dark room within. Climate tells us to stay where we belong and to do what we have always done. On Sunday (in remoter, smaller villages every other Sunday) the cracked church bell sounds off with an unmelodious Bang! Bang! Bang! A stove in the corner crackles and shines but fails to heat. After the service there are brief greetings on the church doorstep, yet nothing in winter can keep us together for long. That is the virtue and even the beauty of this time of year in northern New Mexico: it isolates and intensifies existence, it creates a landscape and then preserves it by freezing it.

III

Decay can be halted, but only briefly, and then it resumes. It is the negative image of history, and its presence throughout northern New Mexico has long fascinated the wandering photographer, hunting for the essence of Spanish-American rural culture. The relentless progress of ruin and abandonment was interpreted as a kind of romantic growth, something to be recorded and perpetuated before it is too late. There was, in fact, a period after World War II when the landscape of the Sangre de Cristo villages and the upper Rio Grande Valley was seen exclusively as a panorama of crumbling adobe walls, sagging roofs, doorways without doors, abandoned roads bordered by rusty barbed wire, leading uncertainly to overgrown fields and resurgent forest. There was never a face except the old and defeated, never a sign of continuing life, but many sad pictures of deserted graveyards. This vision, repeated by artists in many other parts of the country, seems in retrospect to have been less a reflection of reality than a way of expressing a nostalgic version of history: a des-

perate, last-minute recording of old and once-cherished values, the New Mexico chapter in that once-popular chronicling of "vanishing America," the old America of small farms and small villages and small hillside fields. We captured on film the ghosts of places not yet entirely dead.

As long as those remnants of an old, nineteenth-century New Mexico survive as more or less recognizable human artifacts they will remind us of the old order—and of an older photographic approach to the rural world. But it is increasingly evident, I think, that Americans, especially young Americans, are beginning to discover the new landscape that is evolving, demanding our attention and interpretation, if not necessarily our critical acceptance. History has started a new chapter, and our vision expands to include the newer landscape.

Actually it is not a new landscape; it is an aspect of the essential New Mexico landscape—hitherto empty and forbidding—that has been explored, invaded, and occupied. In the last generation we have, for the first time, ventured out beyond the familiar, protective landscape of watered valleys and forested mountains, beyond the green landscape of rain and snow and the traditional succession of seasons, and have undertaken the settlement of the semiarid plains, the naked mountains, and the deserts of the Southwest.

Desert is not a word people in New Mexico like to hear carelessly used. It hurts us deeply to read in eastern papers references to the "desert" around Santa Fe, or the "desert" climate of Albuquerque. No offense is intended, of course. The term conjures up a pleasant image of silence and mystery and strange beauty, and its use is a carry-over from the writings of early nineteenth-century explorers who believed that desert began somewhere in eastern Kansas. To them any region without trees and not adapted to traditional eastern methods of farming was desert. Much of New Mexico, in fact, can be called arid or semiarid—an immense, rolling, underpopulated country covered by short, wiry grass, which in the early summer turns the color of straw.

Geologically speaking, much of eastern New Mexico is an extension of the High Plains—of the Texas Panhandle and Oklahoma. But what distinguishes it from that impressively monotonous region is its variety of landforms—innumerable, widely scattered, dark, steep-sided mesas, floating on the sea of pale yellow grass like a fleet of flat-tops riding at anchor; the cones of extinct volcanoes; the many canyons. These last are remote and hidden from view, and those who formerly explored the rangeland on horseback rather than from the air came upon them with frightening suddenness. All that betrays their existence is a scanty fringe of piñon and juniper on their rim. You find yourself gazing down into a long, deep, narrow valley with almost vertical walls of red or brown rock, and below where you halt there are the tops of cottonwood growing hundreds of feet along some meandering river.

These enormous landforms are about the only variety the arid (or semiarid) landscape of New Mexico provides. In the spring, long after the winter snows have melted and left pools of clear water in the hollows of the rangeland, the grass is a brilliant green, and the expanses of wildflowers—there are said to be more than six thousand varieties in the state—are spectacular. But much depends on when you see the eastern region. If in April, it seems to be potentially ideal farming country; in July it is a sunbaked emptiness, to be avoided whenever possible. Those of us who live here the year round are well aware of the seasonal change. Our lives, like all lives, revolve around the man-made elements in the landscape. We shuttle between people and places—specific people and the specific places where they live and work and relax,

and the expressionless solitudes of the open road between let us say Vaughn and Roswell, or Tucumcari and Hobbs or Logan occupy—or used to occupy little of our thought. We learned to welcome almost every trace, every sign, no matter how incongruous or unsightly, that reminded us of the human presence: the lonely, two-pump gas station, the gate and cattle-guard entrance to some far-off invisible ranch, the tattered billboard out in the middle of nowhere. We were (and perhaps still are) attracted to ruins, no matter what their size or age. Their shabbiness served to bring something like a time scale to a landscape, which for all its solemn beauty failed to register the passage of time.

The story of the dying of small rural communities in every part of the world has become familiar to us all over the last century and a half. It is most impressive, most regrettable when it tells of the decay of a well-known and well-loved landscape, like that of New England or New Mexico, but the moral of the story is in almost every case the same: existence for people in the country became more and more difficult, more and more joyless and without reward. Low pay, monotonous work, a sense of being isolated and forgotten, a sense of diminishing hope for the future afflicted one village, one farmstead after another. For more than a century, here in America, we have seen it happening, so perhaps it is not too early for us to look elsewhere in the countryside to become aware of the new communities, the new installations that are evolving in that rural landscape. If much of the migration from that landscape has found its way to large cities, much of it, perhaps most of it has swelled the population of small towns and even created entirely new types of settlement—still rural in location, but essentially industrial or commercial in economy, dependent not on a stream or river or a climate of familiar seasons, but on a highway, a dam, a mine, a tourist attraction. The movement away from the countryside is everywhere, but in our relatively empty landscape, the fluidity is more easily discerned, and in New Mexico we can, when we look, see more than the decline and death of the traditional order. We can see the emergence, all over the state, of a new kind of community—new in that it represents a different relationship with the environment, a deliberate confrontation with elements in the landscape that earlier generations sought to avoid.

Like many such revolutions, this radical change in settlement patterns was inspired more by hope than despair: hope that a better way of life would come when the steady job was seen as preferable to the exploitation of land, particularly the modest-sized holding of land. The shift got under way in earnest at the time of the depression and the drought of the 1930s. It was then that small farmers and ranchers and farm laborers gravitated to those towns and centers where there was a prospect of work or of some sort of welfare. County seats usually offered some promise of help, and the advent of the unemployed produced a ring of small, inconspicuous shanty towns or Hoovervilles—crude and presumably temporary dwellings, which represented the first visible rejection of the traditional, land-oriented adobe house. These emergency settlements, usually located near the railroad tracks or on vacant lots in the Spanish-speaking neighborhoods, have long since disappeared, replaced by more permanent structures or deserted in favor of other, more suitable public housing projects. Survivals, scarcely recognizable, can still be found on the outskirts of Albuquerque and Santa Fe and Grants, and in other smaller towns. But even if they were short lived, these emergency communities testified to the existence of a new relationship with the landscape: the dwelling, and even the community, moved to be near the source of employment, in contrast to the traditional relationship where employment centered on the dwelling and the land.

Another reason for the proliferation of new settlement types was the advent, after the depression and beginning with the war, of new industries, new construction projects, and numerous military installations throughout New Mexico—oil in the southeastern quadrant of the state, gas in the Farmington area, increased mining in the Gila region. The airfields and army posts attracted a working population to parts of New Mexico that had hitherto been little settled, and when we look back over the last decades we are struck by the manner in which the emptier and less inviting areas have become integrated into the new landscape. It was not merely a matter of discovering and exploiting natural resources of a kind earlier generations had ignored; it was also a discovery of a new way of living, a new environmental relationship. How else are we to account for the new popularity of the snow-bound, wintry landscape of the northern mountains, the attraction of the desert for resort or retirement living? It is true that technological advances have helped to make the remoter regions livable: air conditioning, new, rapid and relatively inexpensive forms of housing—notably the mobile home—and the building of gas lines, airports, and highways have all encouraged the new kind of pioneering, but there have been other forces at work. It is significant that the average prosperous New Mexico suburb has forsaken the familiar valley environment with its cottonwoods and fields of corn and alfalfa for the rocky and treeless heights and mountain slopes: the desirable environment no longer involves the exploitation of land; it is an environment of isolation and extensive views, with few reminders of the traditional community based on agriculture.

The same invasion of the arid or desert environment has taken place in Arizona and California. Wherever we can, we seek out a fresh, untried, unknown setting and impose a new technology upon it, a new awareness of environmental factors, and permanence. Local attachments and identification are not always what we are after: resources can and probably will be exhausted; tastes will change; and better jobs will lure us to another part of the desert or the mountains, or even back to the city. What New Mexico seems to offer is what it has always offered: the dramatic confrontation between the new and mobile and optimistic human installation on the one hand, and the overpowering "timelessness" of an ancient landscape with its visible cosmic chronology on the other—Los Alamos on the flanks of an extinct volcano, the array of lightning rods near Quemado, the clocklike precision of modern irrigation techniques in a region where seasons scarcely exist. The uranium country near Laguna and Grants can be seen as a sample—and not a very happy one—of the new landscape. It is now idle and without movement; perhaps it never will be active again. But it is here that the photographer, seeking to record the new relationship with the environment, can find the most revealing evidence. Mountains have been carved into stepped pyramids and in places planted with bright green grass; the vast piles of waste and slag are, in fact, more natural in appearance than the natural landforms themselves. Model workers' villages, strikingly Mediterranean in style, alternate with villages of mud and rock. Both kinds of community are languishing, each in its way evolving into ruins. The fine paved roads are empty of traffic. The immediate background of this enforced still life is the old grazing landscape of sheep and cattle raising, of half-dead Spanish villages and the deceptively classical, piñon-covered hills and sunbaked rock. Beyond that is the horizon of dark blue mountains. All New Mexico can be seen, superimposed and blending.

The photographer who explores the last landscape—whether in the Four Corners region or in the farmlands of Clovis and Hobbs, or even in the lower Rio Grande Valley—will record in a fresh and direct manner the immensely significant change in environmental relationships, typical of much of the Western world. It is by no means the first such change, nor the last. The prehistoric Indian migrants produced on a modest scale the same juxtaposition of the primordial and the human; the Spanish farmers and ranchers produced their own traditional European version. The drama of New Mexico's attraction and conquest is being continued, and we are in the fortunate position of being able to observe and record that wave of optimistic expansion and discovery. It is no less a fact of history than the compromise and defeat that ultimately overtake our endeavors to live in a region which continues to fascinate us, allure us, and teach us the hard lessons of the passage of time.

1983

Hungo Pavi to Fajada Butte, Chaco Canyon, Edward Ranney

Star Axis, looking South, 1/7/83, Edward Ranney (earth sculpture under construction by Charles Ross)

Archaeological dig, Washington Avenue Development, Santa Fe and *Adobe construction,* near Santa Fe, Richard Wilder

First Comes the House

Along with its other attractions, the Southwest contains the oldest, the least known, and in point of extent the largest countryside of other than English origin in the United States: the Spanish-American. Oldest because it started to evolve in the last years of the sixteenth century; largest because it stretches from the Mexican border well into Colorado, from the Texas Panhandle to the Pacific; least known (and most elusive) because it occupies only a minute fragment of this area and can very well be missed by the traveler passing through. Though inhabited by more than a million people, this landscape is not continuous, and never has been; even in northern New Mexico, the part longest settled, it is a vast scattering of towns, villages, and farms among the mesas and semiarid plateaus, sometimes strung close together along bright green valleys, sometimes hidden in forest-covered mountains or out in the open rangeland; a wide-flung archipelago. Each year the fragments grown smaller and fewer as a more modern American landscape presses against them; on the other hand, as a result of this abandoning of the back country, many new Spanish-American communities have grown up in the last decades on the outskirts of the larger towns. The landscape has to be discovered; like a jigsaw puzzle it has to be assembled before it can be appreciated.

It is worth the effort, however. The loyalty of these small communities to what is to them a valued way of life, their persistence, is something the average American has few chances of seeing. Except for the most meager contacts, they have been cut off for generations from their cultural origins and sources of renewal; and for more than a century they have been immersed in a very different kind of society. Yet somehow they have managed to keep alive much of their Spanish Colonial tradition; its religion, its language, and its architecture.

It is the architecture which is the most conspicuous feature of the Spanish-American landscape, and its nucleus—though architecture is perhaps too imposing a word for these modest farm and village dwellings, small churches, and places of work. You will find no sophistication of design here (which does not prevent many earnest amateurs from seeking it), no remarkable ingenuity of construction, and only a few simple variations on one or two basic forms. It would be more accurate, I think, to speak of rural Spanish-American house-type, because we would thereby exclude the churches, which like all such edifices belong in a class by themselves. However labeled, this country architecture is something unique in the United States: built by local skills—frequently by the occupants themselves—out of local materials, in response to local conditions, almost entirely unaffected by architectural developments in other parts of the nation, and doggedly loyal to a tradition now several centuries old. And a further unusual feature of the style is that it shows every sign of enduring. In all Spanish-American communities, whether in the remotest valley or outside the larger cities, countless examples are being erected every year, each of them true in every essential to the prototype. Indeed it could almost be said that these newest specimens are the best ones to study, since they reveal their structure and purpose without the picturesque increments of time. When therefore we investigate a genuine Spanish-American dwelling—it does not matter of what age—we are not simply investigating as archeologists would an ancient type of structure with an antiquarian appeal; we are investigating a form created by a living society and an expression of that society. That is what makes the Spanish-American house, for all its primitiveness, so vital a topic for study: it shows as no other house-type in the United States does, the link between domestic architecture and the culture which produces it; the link between the single house and the community; and it points the way to how eventually to evaluate architecture of a greater and more enduring kind.

Distribution

The basic task of defining the characteristics of the Spanish-American house-type is in one respect made easy: its distribution coincides very neatly with the distribution of Spanish-Americans throughout the Southwest. This relationship is not so obvious as it might appear; few house-types in Europe, for instance, are identified with any one ethnic or linguistic group. Anglo-Americans are now in the majority in the Southwest, and it might be supposed that they would have adopted a form of dwelling well suited to the region. But they remain loyal to their own inherited house-type and have not taken to the local style in its pure form. They admire it, to be sure, and try to copy it and improve on it, and have adapted it to every conceivable purpose—from football stadiums to powerhouses; but they show a great reluctance to live in a genuine, unmodified specimen, and rarely if ever build an authentic one; the whole concept is foreign to them. So the Spanish-American house flourishes undisturbed, chiefly in the Spanish-speaking communities of the upper Rio Grande and its tributaries, along portions of the San Juan, in the Gila Valley of Arizona, and in southern and western Texas. To the south it merges imperceptibly into the Mexican house-type of Coahuila, Chihuahua, and Sonora, which in fact it often resembles to the point of confusion. It is in Mexico that we will undoubtedly have to look for the origin of many features of the style.

Materials

Ask anyone to define the Spanish-American house in one word, and ten to one he will answer "adobe." While it is certainly true that most of them *look* as if they were made of adobe brick, that is because they have been covered with adobe plaster; many of them underneath are either stone or wood. Wood—in the form of logs or slabs or even railroad ties—is much used in the mountain communities where the forests provide unlimited amounts of timber; the walls are chinked and plastered with adobe to keep out the weather. Stone is favored where there is an easy supply of loose rock of suitable size and shape,

14

cascading down from the disintegrating rimrock above. The stone is never dressed and is simply laid up in the same adobe which later provides the exterior plaster. Some students maintain that there are actually fewer houses of adobe brick in the Spanish Southwest than there are houses of wood or stone. The assertion may be wrong, but it at least indicates that the house-type cannot really be identified with any one material. And even the use of an exterior adobe plaster is by no means universal; it is a practice largely confined to the colder and moister areas. At the risk of confusing the issue, I suggest that the house made of adobe bricks is actually the original, basic southwestern form; the first Spanish Colonial settlers brought with them the technique of making and using adobe bricks, and they settled in river valleys where the soil was suitable to their manufacture. Moreover, most of the settlers came from central Mexico where dwellings of stone or wood were not common. Some believe that the colonists in the Southwest borrowed the house-type of their Pueblo Indian neighbors; aside from the fact that a group no more suddenly "borrows" a house-type than it suddenly "borrows" a language, the Spanish colonists came well prepared to build their own dwellings. Moreover, they brought with them the chimney, something unheard of in the prehistoric Southwest, as an indication of their competence.

Techniques

There is always a risk of attaching too much importance to this question of materials. A frontier society, possessing only the simplest of tools and restricted in its movements to a small area, will naturally use the materials nearest to hand and easiest to process. What actually determines the kind of house built is less the material than the skill and preference of the builder: the human element. If, for instance, these same settlers had somehow found themselves in a humid landscape, they undoubtedly would have made their houses of wood, but they would have built essentially the same kind of house that we know; they would have used their traditional building technique, as we all do. This Spanish-American technique is the post-and-lintel, briefly defined as a form of construction based on the principle of a horizontal member (lintel) supported by a fixed vertical member (post) at either end. In terms of a house, this means a flat, inert roof supported by solid walls. It makes no use of lateral thrusts or interplay of structural forces; it achieves stability through massiveness. It is a static kind of construction, or to use a more inclusive word, it is tectonic: it is obedient first of all to the laws of gravity; roof is supported by wall, wall is supported by foundation, foundation by the earth. The predominant feeling is horizontal, and the bearing walls are always distinct from their load, the roof. Tectonic construction is simple but effective, and it is capable of producing extremely impressive results: Greek architecture of the Classic period was based almost entirely on post-and-lintel methods. Our own happens to be entirely different; whether we are building with stone or wood or reinforced concrete we favor a system based on a frame or skeleton, and the dynamic interplay of members, with walls and roof interlocking. But that has little or nothing to do with the materials we use. For that matter there is nothing in the nature of adobe to make a tectonic system preferable; actually adobe, imaginatively used, can be a most versatile medium; it is capable of a great variety of forms and surfaces—as we can see for ourselves in the architecture of the Mediterranean region and the Near East, of Mexico, and in the prehistoric remains of South America; domes, arches, vaults, towers, subtleties of detail and modeling are all within its range. The Spanish-American builder has always rejected these possibilities. I do not mean to imply that he should have adorned his dwelling with cupolas; but in a land where beams for spanning openings are hard to come by, he would have found the arch a very practical solution. Yet there is not one specimen of the arch dating from Colonial times in the region—except in the Mission churches. It is this sort of evidence—and there is plenty of it—which justifies us in supposing that there is a definite preference in the Spanish Southwest for a static, tectonic construction technique; and this is just as true of the newest houses as of the old: they are all essentially post-and-lintel structures. Why one group evolves one method and remains faithful to it, while its neighbor evolves quite another one, is a large question; construction techniques of the greatest ingenuity have been developed by some of the most primitive societies. The most that we can do, I think, is to recognize that these differences exist, and try to spot them. The average specimen of the Spanish-American house is without attic, without cellar, and sometimes even without a stone foundation; adobe bricks are occasionally laid directly on the bare ground which, enclosed, becomes the bare floor. The roof is supported by beams laid across the narrow dimension of the house and covered with an insulating layer of adobe. Although it appears absolutely flat, it usually has a slight pitch; rain or melted snow drains off through tin or wooden spouts which project far enough to prevent the pouring water from eroding the adobe walls. The roof beams, usually of peeled pine, are perhaps the most valuable and durable elements in the entire structure; in the old days they cost considerable effort to cut, haul, prepare, and put in place; now they cost considerable money. When a house is abandoned, therefore, they are taken away and put to use elsewhere; the rest of the house is allowed to crumble, since few builders will go to the trouble of redeeming the adobe bricks from the ruin.

Plan

Material is not much of an indication of a house-type; building technique is a far better one, but to date we know little about it; best of all is its plan. By plan I mean the layout of the rooms and their interrelationships, and also the manner in which the house grows—an aspect of the subject which architectural historians have paid little attention to. One feature of the southwestern plan is the almost universal absence of a second story. There are, of course, good structural reasons for this: a second story calls for unusual skills in the building of a staircase, in laying floors, in reinforcing walls and ceiling; and a plentiful supply of dressed timber. It has its planning implications too: a second story is only needed when there is a domestic organization complex enough to warrant two separate layouts of rooms. The one-story house was long considered by Anglo-Americans as socially inferior; but now that our domestic architecture has in a sense abandoned the second floor except where space is at a premium, we have begun to look at the two or more story dwelling with a critical eye, and to find hitherto unsuspected merits in the Spanish-American house-type.

Now this house is a one-room house; or to put it another way, the house and the room are identical; the room is thought of and designed to be a completely self-sufficient unit with its own corner chimney (or flue), its own door, its own window; plenty of young Spanish-American working couples start married life in a one-room house standing by itself in a yard. They rapidly acquire a second room, it is true, and a third when they think they need it, but each of these additional rooms is pretty much of the same size, and built to be self-sufficient if necessary. Lest we accept this arrangement as normal, we might compare it with our own Anglo-American way of planning a dwelling. When we set out to build we instinctively think first of the house and then subdivide it into rooms, assigning to each of them a separate function. We ingeniously fit them into one another and into the overall form, and connect them by means of corridors, steps, doors, and so on. This can be an intricate job, as any architect will testify, and an astonishing amount of current architectural discussion concerns the most efficient relationship of interdependent spaces; it never occurs to us that they could be treated separately. And the problem becomes even more intricate with us when there is a question of adding a room; this threatens to throw the whole spatial organization out of kilter, and as a result the average Anglo-American family, when it outgrows its original dwelling (or becomes too small for it), prefers to sell and move elsewhere than to try to adapt the house to changed circumstances. And yet we are persuaded that we have developed a flexible, functional house-type, the best in the world! The Spanish-American knows none of these trials.

The Additive Dwelling

Briefly, the distinction between the two types is this: the basic Anglo-American dwelling unit is the *house,* which we subdivide into rooms; the basic Spanish-American unit is the *room* which is eventually added to. Students of rural architecture have devised terms for these two different processes of growth: the "divisive" and the "additive." When the Spanish-American dwelling adds on more and more rooms—and some of the older ones have grown like a game of dominoes, usually in the form of a U or even a hollow square—it does not thereby increase in complexity, or evolve a labyrinthine plan. It simply grows longer. The consequences of this are several: for one thing,

every wall is built as an outside wall. Visitors to the Southwest never fail to admire the remarkable thickness of the interior walls of the Spanish-American houses, and usually ascribe it to a partiality for massive workmanship, or concern for insulation, or protection against Indian raids. What it actually comes from is the custom of building every wall as an outside bearing wall, never as a simple partition. Another consequence of the additive process is that every room has its own separate roof—sometimes higher or lower than that of its neighbors—its own outside door, its own corner fireplace or flue (with its own chimney), and finally its own diminutive facade. Whatever may be the inconveniences of the plan—the necessity for instance of going through every room in order to get from one end of the house to the other—the esthetic results are usually delightful; the rooms are not deformed as ours so often are by protruding closets and corners and awkwardly placed doors; they are plainly rectangular, with a pleasing location of door and window in the center of the walls, and a sense of each room being an independent space, designed entirely for the convenience of its occupant, not for everyone else in the household. The facade on the additive houses is apt to be long and low and with a vaguely classical formality, thanks largely to the uniform spacing of the windows and doors, the even arrangement of the protruding water spouts, and the lack of ornamentation. There is no attempt at symmetry, no emphasis on a central axis; merely a repetition of more or less identical units of bays, whose monotony is relieved by the slight variations in height. And often, as if to emphasize the autonomy of the separate rooms, one of them will be abandoned, windows broken, roof beams gone, while its neighbors are still inhabited and carefully maintained. But I must repeat: this harmony derives from no architectural instinct; it is simply the happy outcome of the additive process.

House into Village

The question of how the Spanish-American house grows eventually involves the layout of the community, and that is not part of my topic. But the additive process in the course of time produces a communal yard with the communal well in the middle. Translated into urban terms, this is a miniature plaza; in a rural setting it is still a domestic space; though a congeries of such extended houses produces a very urban layout of squares and narrow roads and impressive facades, even when the houses are essentially farmhouses.

Isolation

There is one final visible characteristic to be mentioned, and like the others it is an obvious one. The Spanish-American house, whether of one room or several, prefers to stand off by itself. It prefers a degree of isolation not only from its neighbors but from its own dependent buildings—corral, barn, storehouses, etc. Offhand it would seem a more practical arrangement (in a lonely and unpredictable region) to have the work area close to and even adjoining the dwelling; and such is the common one in most parts of the world, but evidently the Spanish-American farmer or rancher—and housewife—will have none of this intimacy: dwelling remains dwelling, not a place for storing crops and equipment, sheltering animals, or doing farm chores. This trait accounts in part for the proliferation of sheds and storehouses in many Spanish-American establishments: they have all been excluded from the dwelling. It is in fact remarkable to see how scrupulously this division between the two separate aspects of rural life is honored; the dwelling is surrounded by a kind of no-man's land, a neutral zone respected by both parties.

There is no spilling over of domestic life and activity into the outdoors. The well, the oven for baking bread, the clothes line—and perhaps the flowerbed—require the housewife to leave her kitchen, but the family rarely gathers out of doors for sociability or common tasks. It is not a question of climate; the nearby Pueblo Indians transact all kinds of domestic activities outside, from preparing and cooking and eating food, to drying crops on the roof and passing leisure hours there. But it is clear that the Spanish-American house has an entirely different role to play, perhaps even a more important one. The familiar dictum therefore that the farmhouse is an agricultural implement has only a limited truth in the Spanish Southwest. The dwelling is not identified with the work of its inhabitants, and you will examine it in vain for some indication of the kind of farming or ranching its occupant is engaged in. It is, to repeat, essentially a dwelling; its thick walls mark the boundary between two worlds, two different kinds of experience. That, perhaps, is why it is so easily transplanted to an urban environment.

Conservatism

What do these various characteristics add up to? The use of local materials, a predominantly tectonic, post-and-lintel type of construction, the room as the basic unit with an additive form of expansion, and physical isolation and remoteness from the work areas: how do these traits define in any recognizable manner a specific house-type? And no less important, what do they tell about the people who developed it?

Surely their survival indicates a remarkably consistent conservatism, a reluctance to adopt new forms and methods. The way in which the Spanish-American house has

pretended to assimilate certain features of Anglo-American architecture is revealing. About a century ago the pitched frame roof and the porch came to rural New Mexico with the introduction of commercial sawmills and the advent of a permanent Anglo-American population. How long it took those two novelties to be accepted by country people it would be hard to say; but the fact is that the majority of Spanish-American dwellings in the mountains, or wherever there is a supply of timber, now have both gabled roofs and porches running the length of the facade. An indication, you would say, that the style is changing; not at all! Neither of these innovations has been allowed to alter the basic house, or to expand it beyond its traditional boundaries; the space under the gabled roof is rarely used for living; it has its curtained dormer windows, but only a steep outside staircase leads to it, and it serves as an airchamber or storage space. Why then build a gabled roof? To protect the *real* roof from rain and snow. Likewise the front porch, so essential a feature of Anglo-American life, has never become a place where Spanish-Americans spend their idle hours; what it is, is a convenient outside corridor to connect the row of doors in time of snow or rain. Behind the brightly painted porch, underneath the gabled roof, the traditional adobe house, the row of separate cubicles, persists, in no way changed by the wooden additions; rip them off and the routine of existence in the house is in no way altered.

But this conservatism has its healthy and creative aspects; it has in fact perpetuated a type of dwelling which is within reach of every family, no matter how poor; it demands no expensive materials, or special skills and tools. Whenever therefore we lament the absence of originality or refinement, the absence above all of skilled workmanship in these houses we must in justice recognize that these are the inevitable characteristics of a thoroughly democratic house-type. Had the Southwest developed a group of skilled craftsmen—masons, carpenters, plasterers, stone cutters, decorators—the local house-type might well have flowered into a genuine architecture; but it would also have died out, its craftsmen lured away to industry or to the large cities. As it is, the uncompromising conservatism of the style has been its salvation. To be sure, the house-type has assimilated the cement block, though chiefly because of its similarity to the adobe brick; but once let the style become complex, dependent on the skills of specialists, and it will vanish in a generation. It is ironic that the well-meant attempts of certain groups to "revive" the style and give it status may well have just this effect.

Conservatism, though a different sort, accounts for the persistence of the room as a basic unit. We must go to Mexico, I suspect, for a final explanation of the characteristic; it possibly originated in an economy without livestock; on the other hand, it was possibly inherited from the days when the small farmers and ranchers of New Mexico had few possessions and no property. The strictly domestic function of the Spanish-American dwelling suggests that it is more identified with the family than with the land or the work of farming; it is like a shelter where the itinerant farm laborer leaves his family until he can return. One room to a family, to a generation; a row of rooms for a dynasty, a tradition. So the dwelling with room after room, chimney after chimney, door after door, is a symbol of continuity, a living side by side of different generations and conditions, all loosely but effectively joined in loyalty to a family, to the "house" in the genealogical sense of the world. Thus the plan of a building, its gradual expansion (or contraction and abandonment), is largely determined by the evolution of the family, and not by any preconceived architectural scheme. Here again the archaic quality of the Spanish-American dwelling, instead of dooming it, has assured its survival.

19

The Human Factor

Loyalty to primitive (that is, original) forms and techniques is no doubt a trait to be taken into account; it explains much about the style that would otherwise baffle us. But conservatism, after all, characterizes many rural idioms—perhaps most of them. And, indeed, if we are to understand even partially this house-type we must approach it in quite another way. The visible, material qualities are what we have been discussing; the anatomy of the house, as it were. But in the last analysis the house has to be seen as a vehicle of a universal experience, as a sign of how man tries to relate himself to the world surrounding him.

And of all the traits in this particular dwelling that seem to demand human interpretation, I can think of none more suggestive than its isolation; its physical remoteness from neighbors and place of work, its detachment from outdoor activity. Climate, we are told, determines to a large extent the form of the house and the routine of its inhabitants. True; but *which* aspect of the climate? For in the Southwest (as in most other regions of the world) climate has its extremes, and we are obliged to adjust to one or the other, if not to both. The Japanese house, for instance, is designed primarily with the warmer months in mind—even though the Japanese winter is said to be often severe. The same holds true, though to a lesser degree, of the Italian house; it is at its most livable in summer. But this represents a choice, and the Spanish-American house seems to have chosen to meet the challenge of winter. The thick walls, the small and infrequent openings are (to be sure) proof against heat as well as cold; but the low ceilings, the compartmentalization of the interior, the absence of through currents of air, and the total neglect of the roof as a place of resort—even, I should say, the generally secluded location of the house itself—all seem to suggest that the chief preoccupation of the builder has been to insulate human life against wind and cold and snow and other harsh aspects of the environment. It is attitudes of this sort toward environment, rather than the environment itself, which influence the form of the dwelling.

Our own Anglo-American enthusiasm for a merging of the outdoors and indoors, of work and play, of private and public life, is so uncompromising, so much (it seems to us) a reason for self-congratulation, that it is next to impossible to realize that another society may not share it; and thus we ascribe any resistance to the custom to a kind of conservatism which time will overcome. But the resistance on the part of the Spanish-Americans (like the same resistance in other Latin cultures) is, I believe, something much more positive than a mere prejudice. It derives as I see it from a specific, well-formulated, and long-established concept of the dwelling.

Almost from the beginning, the colonists in the Southwest, to the distress of the Colonial authorities, displayed a reluctance to live in compact or organized villages even when their safety was at stake. Community living had little appeal to them, and it is significant that their house-type never evolved anything approaching an urban style. Except, perhaps, for the addition of a second story, the houses in nineteenth-century Santa Fe were identical with those in the smallest hamlet; and if the dwellings are sometimes clustered in the rural areas this is chiefly because they must all share a limited water supply. This refusal to blend with the group or with the natural surroundings would seem to be an expression of a basic belief that there are two worlds: the inside world of the individual and his family, concentrated in the dwelling, and an outside world of society and work and nature; and that they are to be kept separate.

It must be some such conviction that has inspired an

unusual intensity of feeling for the house—especially the interior—in the rural Southwest. This has been kept alive by two things: the occupants of the dwelling—man and wife—have usually built at least one room of it themselves; mixed and molded and laid the adobe bricks, raised the roof beams, and plastered the walls. The other must also be the satisfaction of properly conforming to a widespread and respected tradition, of duplicating with only minor variations the kind of dwelling both of them had known in childhood, the dwelling of their ancestors and relations and friends. We who merely buy or rent our houses (and rarely for a lifetime) can never entirely comprehend what this sort of participation means; and even the function of the Spanish-American dwelling undoubtedly escapes us. It is not a status symbol, it is not an investment, it is not part of the business of earning a living; it is a small private world, detached from all mundane concerns; it is almost literally the physical extension of those who built it. The plaster bears the imprint of their hands; the roof beams show the marks of their ax; the walls are measured by their reach, and doors and windows are where instinct told them they needed light. Even the dimensions are not those prescribed by standardized measurements or prefabrication, but by a feel for human proportion. It is certainly not hard to enumerate the shortcomings: the inconvenient planning, the absence of any craftsmanship, of any indication of a formal cultural heritage; but these are the result of excluding the outside world with such finality.

One of the features of the tectonic method of building, it has been said, is its awareness of the human scale and body. It defines structural elements in terms of the body, and the relationship between bearing wall and load is one which man can appreciate in terms of his own muscular strength. This peculiarly human quality carries over into the function of the house itself; for the house symbolizes not work or struggle against nature, or collective history, but a sort of basic humanity. This is the place (it seems to say) where men can close the door on the outside world, and surrounded by their own creation, their own kin, recover their essential human identity. Any house which plays this role inevitably possesses a grace of its own; and that is why Spanish-American dwellings are often so beautiful. Even the poorest and crudest among them can express the dignity of their purpose.

This southwestern house-type is, as I have said, common to something like a million Americans; in a somewhat modified form it is also common to many times that number of Mexicans, and in both countries examples are being built each year in great quantities. Yet not even the most loyal admirer of the type will claim that it is of any great practical significance outside of the Southwest. For all its cheapness and simplicity it is nothing that the rest of the country can imitate. It is for one thing too closely identified with what is to most of us a bygone way of life, an economy and a social order that we have for better or worse outgrown. At a time when more and more Americans are becoming urbanized, when the construction industry is providing us with mass-produced houses designed for rapid obsolescence, there can be little of immediate value in a style of dwelling which still clings to its rural origins and to a concept of the house impossible for us to believe in.

Nevertheless, there is not an American architect or planner, wherever he lives or whatever his practice, who could not benefit by studying the Spanish-American house-type.

Not because it behooves him to become acquainted with the rich variety of the American landscape—as, indeed, it does; but because it would open his eyes to the immensely complex nature of the dwelling and its func-

tion. It would enlighten him to see what a maze of social, technical, geographical, historical, biological traces even the simplest house can be; to learn that other societies have in their time reached different but quite viable solutions to some of the problems confronting him, and that current definitions of architecture, for all their appearance of rationality, may well be based on unconscious preferences for forms and relationships originating far back in our own past.

The disappearance of the owner-built house in American may be a sign of social progress, but it has certainly made us less aware than we used to be of one of the bases of all architectural development; the efforts of the individual man to come to terms with his social and natural environment. We have tended, in consequence, to forget that the house, the simplest and most human of all architectural forms, has always come first. The unique value of the Spanish-American landscape to the rest of America lies here: it reminds us of the basic individual and human aspects of architecture and its kindred arts.

Landscape 9, no. 2 (Winter 1959–60): 26–32.

The Swallow's House, Progresso, Meridel Rubenstein

Rio Lucio, Alex Harris

The sheep camp at Mesita in Laguna Pueblo, Meridel Rubenstein

Truchas, Alex Harris

Zia Pueblo, Paul Logsdon

27

Chetro Ketl, Chaco Canyon, Paul Logsdon

28

Pueblo Dwellings and Our Own

The territory occupied by the prehistoric Pueblo culture can be briefly described as the immense, scantily populated plateau country centering on the Four Corners where New Mexico, Arizona, Utah, and Colorado touch. It is uniformly high—the elevations of the Pueblo villages range from 5,000 to 8,000 feet—and its rainfall is seldom more than fifteen inches a year. The Hopi villages of Arizona survive on less than eleven inches. By contrast the rainfall of eastern New England is about forty-three inches.

There are few perennial streams, though small springs are numerous, and the landscape is a vast and colorful panorama of mesas and canyons and broad valleys. Except in the few spots favored with water, the vegetation is harsh and thin, but no village is more than forty or fifty miles from mountains with stands of pine and spruce and aspen, and an abundance of game. The dry and sunny climate, punctuated by brief violent storms, is remarkably healthy.

For all its common environmental characteristics the area has enormous diversity. It includes the hot lower Rio Grande Valley where frosts are all but unknown and the growing season is long, as well as the cool foothills of the Sangre de Cristos. There are half-hidden valleys with fertile soil and flowing rivers, and in the western part wide plains choked by rock and sand. In any Old World region of similar extent we would see a great regional variety of cultural landscapes, no two of them alike, but in the prehistoric Southwest, cultural variations are surprisingly few, and variations in architecture even fewer. "The essential uniformity of [building] types which prevails over the immense area covered by the ancient Pueblo ruins," Mindeleff remarks, "is a noteworthy feature, and any system of classification which does not take it into account must be considered as only tentative."*

Since those words were written, more than ninety years ago, archeology and ethnographic fieldwork have revealed the existence of several ethnic or historical subregions, and Mindeleff himself was aware of several distinct kinds of settlement patterns. Yet the overall uniformity of prehistoric house-types is still recognized as a significant characteristic of the whole landscape.

---

*Cosmos Mindeleff: "Cliff ruins of Canyon de Chelly, Arizona," *Sixteenth Annual Report of the Bureau of American Ethnology. 1894–95.*

How is such uniformity to be explained? In the nineteenth century scholars assumed that it was the result of environmental factors: that identical or similar climates, topography, and natural resources produced identical or similar kinds of dwellings. They had a point, but we now realize that there are also social factors to take into account. The social, economic, and political—and even legal—character of a community has much to do with the local house-type. Weather and terrain are, of course, influential, but when we build a house and use locally available skills and locally available materials, when we conform to local ideas as to the role of the dwelling and relationship with neighbors and with the place of work, when we undertake to respect the spirit of the village itself, we are in fact conforming to the local house-type. The rewards for this kind of conformity are often very satisfactory: a sense of belonging to the village, of membership. The Pueblo communities of the prehistoric Southwest, like most isolated and autonomous farm villages, attached great value to homogeneity. All of them observed much of the same public rites and ceremonies, lived by the same fixed agricultural and religious calendar, and all were dedicated to preserving the same intricate social order. In consequence, the dwellings of the prehistoric Pueblo Indians were similar to one another, not only in each individual village but throughout the region.

A standard type of vernacular dwelling, primarily for working people, is a fairly common phenomenon, and indeed becoming even more common as public authorities undertake to provide dwellings on a wholesale scale. But what we are likely to find impressive about the southwestern version is that its uniformity rarely suggests enforced compliance, or even a conscious desire to conform. No matter how similar they may all be as to shape and size and construction, the prehistoric Pueblo dwellings somehow manage to tell us that each is an individual achievement—the private, almost instinctive expression of what must be an ancient prototype. To the European-American student, Pueblo architecture is extremely hard to understand, which perhaps is why we have never really tried. The prehistoric dwelling is *not* architecture, and it is modest enough to invite speculation. Unlike the larger and more imposing prehistoric collective structures, it allows us to compare our own ways of building with those of a vanished culture. One mystery confronted can lead to the recognition of others.

It is generally agreed that the basic unit in Pueblo architecture is the room. Since the width of a room is determined by the length of the roof beams, we rarely find a room much wider than fourteen feet, and a room of twelve by twenty would be accounted large. Many rooms, possibly used for storage, are no more than five feet square. When it is said that this boxlike room or cell is the basic structural unit, we mean that no larger or more complex unit of construction was ever devised, and indeed the room is the equivalent of the dwelling in its simplest form. But paradoxically enough, this basic unit is never self-sufficient. It must always be related to a row or collection of similar units, which is perhaps the equivalent of saying that the *dwelling* as the domicile of the nuclear family is never self-sufficient, but viable only when it is used in conjunction with other domiciles, other rooms occupied by members of the extended family, or clan, all centered on a family shrine.

The second implication of this definition of the room as basic unit is this: every Pueblo building, no matter what its size, is actually nothing more than a cluster of such cells. Even the largest community house, like the one at Taos, six stories high and a quarter of a mile long, is a honeycomb of innumerable small, rectangular rooms. It may be objected that this is also true of every modern

European-American building: are they not all essentially clusters of cells of varying dimensions? Yes, but they are designed and constructed as a complex unit subsequently divided. The frame, the armature comes first with us; with the prehistoric Pueblo builder the cell or room comes first and is then duplicated. One of the most valuable insights into the nature of Pueblo architecture is Whorf's comment that the Hopi language contains no word for *room.* "We are struck by the absence of terms for interior three dimensional spaces, such as our words 'room, chamber, hall, passage' . . . in spite of the fact that Hopi buildings are frequently divided into several rooms, sometimes specialized for different occupancies."* Is it possible that we, no less than the Hopis, are unconscious victims of our language when we attempt to interpret architecture? We are almost incapable of perceiving the dwelling as other than a collection of rooms. We even speak of a one-room house, as if the room were somehow distinct from the *interior* of the house. And yet this notion does not carry over into our way of seeing other interior three-dimensional spaces: we do not have a word for the interior of a bottle or a drawer or a glass. The Hopi are more consistent in this respect: they see the house as a receptacle; its interior is temporarily defined in terms of its temporary content. "The Hopi," Whorf continues, "do not use occupancy terms as synonymous with the term for the building housing the occupancy. . . . The occupancy of a piki-house is called by a term which means 'place where the griddle is set up' but it would be called that if set up outdoors, and there is no term for the piki-house itself."

---

*Benjamin Lee Whorf: "Linguistic factors in the terminology of Hopi architecture," in *Language, Thought and Reality.*

A Pueblo room (or basic dwelling) is thus nothing more than a three-dimensional interior space, a receptacle (to repeat) in which objects are contained or events occur. The room itself imposes no identity on its temporary contents, and in turn the contents do not permanently characterize the room. Only a collection, a sequence of rooms can have that effect. It is as if the occupants were saying that the single space, the single event is of no consequence: it is *repetition* which creates the periodic or rhythmic recurrence of spaces and events, the cosmic order.

The rectangular, flat-roof building, call it dwelling or room or receptacle, is made of stone or adobe or a combination of the two. We tend to associate it with adobe, but there is good evidence that stone was preferred. Some authorities believe that several prehistoric communities knew how to form adobe into something like bricks. But in the great majority of structures the adobe was compacted into balls or wads and put in place, course by course, without the addition of straw or any binding agent. Walls thus constructed were likely to be fragile and easily eroded by rain. The stone walls were frequently laid up without mortar, smaller stones being wedged into the cracks and spaces. Adobe was also used to close the chinks, but this could occur only after a rain had provided water to make mud.

The typical foundation is rarely excavated, and usually consists of a row of rocks and stones posed on the surface of the site. The roof beams—logs of aspen, spruce, or pine brought with some labor from the nearest forest—are peeled, but never dressed or squared. A peculiarity of the dwelling is that is has no door leading to the outside on the ground floor, but is entered by means of a trapdoor in the roof, and a ladder. The effect must be to transform the ceiling into a surface connected with the world; not a distinct element in the room but a continuation of the walls on another plane: the sense of containment, or stereotomic space, is reinforced.

All of these materials are the product of the local environment—a very restricted environment in that the Pueblo Indians had no beasts of burden. To quote again from Mindeleff,

> One of the peculiarities of Pueblo architecture is that its results were obtained always by the employment of materials immediately at hand. In the whole Pueblo region no instance is known where the material (other than timber) was transported to any distance; on the contrary, it was usually obtained within a few feet of the site where it was used. Hence it comes about that difference in character of masonry is often only a difference of material.

In this connection, therefore, "available" means not only those materials that are easy to carry but that need little or no processing—which is to say that they are not necessarily the strongest or most adaptable materials nor those that last the longest. Whoever has examined Pueblo craftsmanship in their buildings must be aware of the fact that the builders were well acquainted with the properties of the various materials and were capable of extremely precise and beautiful results, particularly in their use of stone. Many of the walls they built show considerable preparation: the choosing of uniform size and texture, the laying of bands of distinct color, and the chinking with small stones often produce what must be a deliberate artistic effect. Indeed it is their concern for smooth and uniform textures that leads the Pueblo builder often to cover a rough stone wall with a coat of adobe. But what one eventually notices is the lack of concern for establishing any bond with the immediate environment, more specifically, the lack of awareness of the natural forces

or processes that will in time threaten the security of the building. It is well known that Pueblo architecture did not use the keystone or the arch, that they did not use the column, and used the buttress with little skill. They often did not build even the slightest foundation. The corners in their masonry houses were never bonded, and a wall supporting three or four stories is often no sturdier than one which supports the roof and roof beams only. Experience must have taught them that thrust and weight, settling and expansion ought to be taken into account, but it was a lesson which they chose to ignore. Why such skillful and ingenious builders should so choose is one of the mysteries of Pueblo culture; one can only surmise that there were some aspects of the natural environment, some forces within it that they could not or would not recognize. "The absence of any attempt to improve the natural advantages of the site is remarkable. No expedients were employed," Mindeleff remarks,

> to make access either easier or more difficult, except that here and there series of hand and footholes have been pecked in the rock . . . the cavities in which the [Canyon de Chelly] ruins occur are always natural; they are never enlarged or curtailed or altered in the slightest degree, and very rarely is the cavity itself treated as a room, although there are some excellent sites for such treatment.

Elsewhere he describes the futile attempts of the builders to use timbers for the foundations of walls.

The world offers us two different ways of interpreting the passage of time and of ordering the time we live by, and here in the Southwest both of them derive from the beauty and immensity of the region. The first way is by observing the annual movements of the heavenly bodies and how those movements create the sequence of days and seasons and the four directions. From the predictable recurrence of summer and winter, night and day, life and death, from the cyclical nature of celestial time we learn to devise a formal social order, an elaborate calendar, and a harmonious way of life that promises to endure forever.

The other way of interpreting time comes from our everyday experience of the world around us, from contact with the earth itself. Here is where we are confronted with uncertainty and constant, unpredictable, irreversible change, which we are powerless to oppose. Whether the events that form and transform our environment are sudden and brief like a flood or the crashing down of a canyon wall, or whether they go on for decades like a drought, their time scale teaches us nothing. Nevertheless it is possible to study it, so that in the course of generations we can understand this earthly system of time and eventually eliminate some of its terrifying and destructive unpredictability.

The prehistoric Pueblo people seem to have chosen that celestial, antihistorical concept of time, and to have given little thought to that other time which ticks off its passage by slow erosion or the widening of a crack in a wall or the crumbling of a foundation. They built as if the present were going to last, untroubled by age and neglect and decay. Benjamin Whorf's exploration of the Hopi concept of time and his essay on Hopi architectural terms is not only a brilliant revelation of the connection between language and notions of time, but a revelation of how our architecture differs from that of the Pueblo Indians.

One radical difference is our European-American reverence for history. Any architectural student who is honest with himself will seek to define a style first of all in historical terms, not by the use of metalinguistics; and in fact he is likely to conclude that the vernacular dwelling of prehistoric and Dark Age Europe had certain similarities with that of the prehistoric pueblos: both types were basic all-purpose rooms, both were receptacles, both were built out of locally available materials, and both were examples of tectonic structures; lastly, according to archeologists on both sides of the Atlantic, neither house-type evolved in any significant manner during a period of more than five hundred years.

But (again according to European archeologists) the vernacular or peasant dwelling in northwestern Europe began, sometime in the tenth and eleventh centuries, to undergo a series of changes, largely in construction; and what these changes seem to have signified is that the European dwelling ceased to be a receptacle, a container, and evolved as a distinct organism, with interior features having no direct connection with the exterior: new types of partition were developed, new forms of framing and joining, the procedure of building in terms of bays, roofs, and walls that resisted the weather more effectively, better foundations that resisted the action of frost, better lighting, better and easier access—all became features of even the simplest dwelling. Some of these improvements were imported from elsewhere; others resulted from the use of better tools or better building materials, but the upshot was that the vernacular house in medieval Europe began to resemble what might be called a counterenvironment: an environment (or microenvironment) deliberately designed to resist the assaults of the world outside and above and underneath. The dwelling became an instrument for work and for the preservation of the family: the interior was seen as distinct from the exterior.

We can leave to one side any attempt to account for this development. The significance I think was that the house became a complex and flexible artifact, largely because it established a new and effective identity as a counterenvironment.

The Pueblo dwelling never did this; perhaps because of a more equitable climate, perhaps because of the total absence of domestic animals, but perhaps also because of a deep-rooted reliance on the house or room as the minimal structure, its use and form were determined more by social than by environmental factors. If it was a question of giving a name to this type of dwelling, it could be termed *protovernacular*—not yet completely vernacular in its dependence on a racial archetype and its lack of a clear-cut distinction, structurally speaking, between exterior form and interior space. It may well be that as we study the prehistoric Pueblo dwelling in more detail we will discover the beginnings of the full-fledged interior, the counterenvironment. Under the influence of European-American examples, the contemporary Pueblo dwelling has already become vernacular; it is, however, no longer true to its tradition of more than a thousand years.

This revised essay originally appeared as "Pueblo Architecture and Our Own," *Landscape* 3, no. 2 (Winter 1953–54): 20–25.

Raton Pass, Joan Myers

High Plains Country

First Sight

A small party of buffalo hunters, trappers, horsemen, and teamsters on the way from Missouri to Santa Fe were the first to celebrate the Fourth of July on New Mexico soil. This was in 1831, and the place was the wide valley of the Corrumpa in the northeasternmost corner of the province. A historical marker stands in what is now someone's winter pasture, not far from farmhouses and a paved highway.

A century and a quarter ago the region was not only foreign, it was lonely and dangerous, and the men were celebrating more than a holiday; they were celebrating their having come through the worst part of their long journey alive, and their now being near the end. They had in fact left behind them the sixty-mile stretch of desert between the Arkansas River west of Dodge City and the Cimarron River in the extreme southwest corner of Kansas—a dry and treeless landscape, more feared by travelers than the Comanches and Apaches who were sometimes seen there. Even the best-equipped of wagon trains suffered from the lack of water, and it was said that one group of men had cut off the ears of their mules, to quench their dreadful thirst by drinking warm blood.

Once reached, the Cimarron usually provided men and animals with water enough. But it was an erratic stream. Here, more than one hundred and fifty miles from its source in the mountains of northern New Mexico, it was less than three feet deep at the best of times. It meandered over a wide bed between sand dunes; during the heat of the day the water vanished, reappearing only after dark. In dry years the flow was little more than a trickle. Travelers on the Santa Fe Trail then avoided what was called the Cimarron Cut-off, preferring the mountain passes and the risk of Indian attacks to the probability of death by thirst.

At Lower Springs where the travelers usually rested overnight, the Cimarron was the watering place for the herds of buffalo which grazed on the plains to the north and south. Waking the next morning, the men were amazed to see the valley below them and for miles in either direction a solid, restless mass of dark and rusty brown buffalo. The great beasts showed no fear; they parted to let the wagons and horsemen cross the river and head westward along the opposite bank, and then closed in once more. Throughout that day and the next buffalo in small bunches were rarely out of sight; neither was the Cimarron River, now flowing between steep banks to the north.

Then the country changed. The trail had gradually climbed as it crossed the plain, and the plain was now covered with a continuous sod of thick grass. The sky ahead became a more vivid blue, and the heat of the midsummer day was tempered by a wind from the south and west. Finally there rose out of the immensity of tawny grass two solitary dark blue peaks; small and far away, and silhouetted against the cloudless sky. How welcome must have been this sight to travelers who for weeks had seen nothing but the plain! It doubtless brought to mind a more familiar landscape of trees growing on hillsides, of shade and abundant streams. To the hot and exhausted men the prospect was still further cause for giving thanks.

Actually the two peaks (as horsemen among the group soon discovered) were eminences of one single mountain—Rabbit Ear Mountain, which rose more than two thousand feet upon a pedestal of mesa and plateau. It had been named for a Comanche chief active in this region in the early eighteenth century until the Spanish militia had pursued and killed him. A naked mass of igneous rock, it was always a significant landmark for westbound travelers, for it meant that New Mexico had at last been reached. Today it is identified with the town of Clayton, the seat of Union County, which lies at its base.

Almost at the spot where Rabbit Ear Mountain had become visible, the landscape acquired another character. There were no longer buffalo; instead the men saw antelope and deer and even wild horses. One after another mountains rose singly out of the plain: peaks and domes and truncated towers, dark with rock even under the bright sun, stood apart from one another, like monuments. Near

at hand there were groves of small cedars and junipers, leading down to the great red walled canyon of the Cimarron a few miles to the north. As the men moved farther into the spacious landscape they were exhilarated and no longer weary; this was the country of horsemen and of hunters. The marvelous honey-colored grass, vigorous underfoot, reached mile after mile over the hills, and down into the shallow valleys; briefly interrupted by the line of black rimrock, it resumed its sweep across the plain to the very foot of the mountains. Not a tree, not so much as a bush broke the expanse. Far to the west, down on the horizon itself, was the Sangre de Cristo range. Snow still gleamed on its peaks under the bright blue sky.

While the wagons moved slowly along the rutted trail from one valley (and one water-hole) to another, always traveling south and west, the horsemen went after the antelope and, with better luck, after the wild horses. Sometimes a brave and expert rider, familiar with the country and its ways, roped a likely mustang, saddled it, and rode it at a wild run across the plain, until the frantic but exhausted animal acknowledged defeat. The exulting horseman rejoined the train at a walk; he had added a new and half-broke mount to his string.

After two days the Canadian River was reached; Santa Clara, the present-day Wagon Mound, and the first Mexican settlement lay another day's journey ahead. The wagons negotiated the river's steep bank; they and the horsemen disappeared, and the dust subsided. Other trains followed, year after year, for many decades; yet none left a mark to remind us of their having passed. Since the last wagons used them, almost a hundred years ago, the ruts have eroded and in places are four feet deep; but to the untrained eye they look like natural features of the landscape. Is it not strange that the Santa Fe Cut-off, so fearsome and adventurous a road in its day, should in a sense be forgotten? No road, not even a trail, follows its course.

Round Mound, Joan Myers

No town or settlement had grown in those places where the wagons stopped for the night. For all that Union County can show, the Santa Fe Trail never crossed it.

Thus is borne out the sensible observation of the geographer Capot-Rey: that no road or trail, however frequently traveled, ever produces a permanent settlement by its mere existence. Only a shift in the means of transportation or an interruption in the journey itself can bring this about; and for all its hardships, the Santa Fe Trail was the path of steady and uninterrupted movement from East to West.

The Lay of the Land

During the first three days of their journey across New Mexico, travelers on the Cimarron Cut-off passed through much of the Union County, from northeast to southwest. But of the county's general aspect they saw very little.

It is in truth a very extensive tract of land; more than fifty miles wide from the Oklahoma and Texas line on the east to Colfax County on the west; sixty miles and more from Colorado on the north down to the Harding County line: in all, 3,817 square miles. That is more than three-quarters the area of the state of Connecticut; but whereas there are on the average more than 400 people to the square mile in Connecticut, out here there are barely two. In 1954 the population of Union County was 5,200 (it was larger by some 6,000 before the Dust Bowl and the depression) and more than half of this number lives in Clayton with a population of 3,450, Des Moines (300), and Folsom (200). This means that most of the county outside of these three places—the largest aggregations—has an average density of less than one person to the square mile.

Translate this into visual terms: the dry farmer and his family living down in the sandy country along the Texas line count as their closest neighbor another dry farmer who lives a mile away possibly out of sight, and there may or may not be another neighbor in the other direction. As for the cattle rancher living farther west, he can gaze from his front door out over five or six miles of range and see nothing but his own windmill, his own cows, his own fence—and then miles more of his neighbor's range on the other side. The size of the average holding in Union County is usually given as five square miles; spacious enough. But since this includes many dry farms of a section (one square mile) each, we can suppose that the average ranch is actually a good deal larger, in some instances ten times larger. So between the various isolated ranch headquarters surrounded by their plantings of Chinese elms and their diminutive lawns there can be and frequently are enormous stretches of unbroken pasture land where no man seems ever to have been.

Often, very often indeed, the High Plains landscape has been likened to a sea of grass. That cannot be helped; the simile is an excellent one, valid in many dimensions. Romantic, as when used by Conrad Richter as the title of his novel about ranching in northeastern New Mexico; critical, as when a cowman damns a pasture for being totally without breaks or shelter against winter storms; prosaic, as when a geographer seeks to descibe an extensive flat and treeless area. Ever since the first white man set eyes on this country the phrase has been in constant use, and it still forces itself upon us. The abrupt and lonely mountains are islands, the rock outcroppings are shoals, the grass itself ripples in waves before the wind, and after a day spent under the bright sun amid the simplicities of a countryside stripped of detail, you half believe that you have in fact been on the sea. You lick your lips for the taste of salt.

So sea of grass it is, and if the figure helps make some part of Union County more vivid, then by all means let it continue to serve—always provided that we think of that sea as full of movement, and further that we suppose the ranchhouses, scattered about in the draws, to be seagulls riding out a storm in the trough of the waves.

But the sea, however vast, covers only part of the county. A strip some twenty miles broad along the northern border includes extremely wild and rugged terrain, as well as the Canyon of the Cimarron. Here among the mesas and cedar breaks and lateral canyons are to be found the highest summits in the county, one of the highest being Emery Peak, near Folsom, with an altitude of 7,350 feet. Off in the deep valleys and the forests to the west, where the snows lie until April, and every canyon has its bear, there is a place known as the Alps—a name which ought to tell us something of the local topography. All this is country to be proud of, and to compare with any other.

No doubt the same can be said of the east side of the county, the area lying beyond the escarpment and parallel to the Texas line. It has its own characteristics: it is composed of sandy soil and great expanses of tall bunch grass and soapweed; rolling country; and unexpectedly, every so often a wide and shallow canyon (without water, of course) comes creeping through the plain. Equally unexpected are the occasional wide and desolate views to the east over hundreds of square miles of more sand and tall grass and soapweed, more canyons growing shallower as they meander. This is not the cheeriest landscape in the world, yet it is probable that many people look upon it with satisfaction; it is here that most of the farms in the county are located.

Taken as a unit, the county slopes from west to east, gradually and almost imperceptibly; from 6,868 feet at Capulin to 5,050 at Clayton, nine miles from the Texas line. No perennial streams rise in Union County, and with the possible exception of the Cimarron River, none flows through its territory. A possible exception because for much of the year the Cimarron has no water, so that it is locally (and quite correctly) known as the Dry Cimarron—perhaps to distinguish it from the much smaller but more active river of the same name which flows into the Canadian farther west in New Mexico. But if the streams are ephemeral the valleys are not. These are of many kinds: hardly discernible grass-grown draws out on the range, winding arroyos bordered by tumbled rocks and piñon trees, dry and sandy streambeds deep below the level of the surrounding land—these lead to the east and south, where all (again excepting the Cimarron) contribute their scanty and unpredictable flow to the Canadian. The Canadian eventually empties into the Arkansas.

If we exclude that immense and spectacular sea of grass—or more scientifically speaking, the many square miles of open range—we will not find one single topographical feature dominating the landscape of Union County. The distant Rockies dwarf all lesser mountains, but they have nothing to do with the local system of drainage. The several valleys and draws and arroyos which cross the county to the east originate not in the Sangre de Cristos but on the slopes of a remarkable group of extinct volcanoes and volcanic remains on the extreme western edge of the county. Some thirty of these, several of which reach 8,000 feet in height, rising out of the open plain near Des Moines give that landscape a distinctly lunar quality. No doubt the Dry Cimarron Canyon excels these cones and craters in grandeur; the canyon is more than 500 feet deep and a good 70 miles long. But for several reasons it has had comparatively little effect on the landscape, human or natural. It has attracted few tributary streams, only one, the Travesser, being of any size. Neither has it attracted the population it deserves. Like the mesa country to the north of it, the canyon remains impressive yet somewhat remote.

Perhaps the county is too large to be identified with any one formation; perhaps it is only the sea of grass which really counts. Once you have left that, whether for a mountain or a canyon or even a volcano as perfect in shape as on the day it last erupted, you have left the true High Plains landscape; abandoned the open sea for what are after all merely islands within it.

Landscape 3, no. 3 (Spring 1954): 11–22.

Melissa Armijo, Eloy Montoya, Richard "El Wino" Madrid, Albuquerque, Miguel Gandert

The Social Landscape

Our relationship with the environment, natural and man-made, has greatly changed in the past fifty years. We used to believe that a truly harmonious relationship would result when man took his identity from his setting. Environmentalism, under one name or another, was a popular doctrine: we were all products of our environment, and so the design and care of the environment was of great importance. Now we have begun to search for identity in other ways; and more and more we are inclined to manipulate the environment, use it as a tool for creating our identity.

The search for identity assumes many forms; one which directly affects the landscape is a growing dependence on other people, a gregariousness. What we are (or think we are) is not simply a matter of what we do and accomplish, but of how we affect others. Just as we say there is no sound unless there is an ear to register it, we also assume that there is no human identity unless there is another person to recognize it. We seem to be redefining man once again as a social animal—though not as a political animal—and recognizing the necessity for communication. Nothing can more vividly illustrate this change than our present attitude toward solitary confinement, as contrasted with the attitude of a hundred and fifty years ago. At that time solitary confinement was not thought of as a punishment, but a speedy and effective type of reform therapy: the individual was confronted with himself and learned what his mistakes had been. He was safe from the contamination of society. Now it is considered the harshest punishment that can be inflicted.

The process of self-definition cannot go on by itself; it calls for the presence of others, and people of the younger generation know this better than anyone else. It is a dialogue, not a monologue, and that is why existential writers in particular attach such importance to language, to communication. Existence means *shared* existence. We are all increasingly dependent on the presence of our fellow men—not necessarily on their approval; their reaction to our existence is just as essential.

The results of this tendency to get together, informally and perhaps briefly, are very evident. Urbanization is one obvious example; but it is visible on a much smaller scale as well. What we are likely to notice, when we look at the social life of the average American small town or city, is that the favorite places of social interaction are not the institutions which previous generations preferred: the church, the public building, the public square, the club or lodge, or the so-called community center or the school. These are no longer popular except on special occasions. We have found other places for meeting together.

A Swiss sociologist* has observed that much contemporary planning theory is actually based on only those needs which we share with animals—shelter, food, recreation, movement, work, or defense. This would certainly be a logical inheritance from the nineteenth century, because it ignores what we now consider our most essentially human trait—our need to communicate, to be social. In any case, without the assistance or guidance of planners we are beginning to establish places for informal social interaction; and these places are well worth study.

If the desire for communication is one of the most important aspects of our drive for self-definition, then the highway is the prime symbol of this drive. Communication can be defined in several ways: it means passage from one place to another, and it means the transmitting of a message. In terms of the highway, it means an unending flow of traffic—perhaps much of it essentially aimless, a kind of search for some place or person to help reinforce our identity; it also means the signs and billboards and lights and signals—a chorus of communications such as no generation has ever before seen. We are told that this confused collection of messages is undermining our sanity, but we somehow contrive to find our way through it. We may not enjoy it, but one virtue of our being communications-minded is that we have learned how to filter out those communications which don't concern us. We deal with the familiar, recognizable symbols.

---

*See Paul Hotz, "Planning of Mice and Men," *Landscape*, 16:2, pp. 12–14.

It is along the highway, particularly in the built-up areas, that we can best see that kind of exhibitionist, self-identifying architecture which is designed to convey as loudly and as vividly as possible some assertion of identity to the passerby—motels, drive-in establishments, shopping centers, even factories and office buildings and churches.

None of these signs and structures possesses an *essential* identity: they seek to establish a kind of existential identity by setting up a brief dialogue: "See me!" they cry; and we answer, "I see you; you're a root beer stand (or a drive-in movie)." They are like those teenagers, more numerous in the West, who wear their identity carved on their belts or on the backs of their jackets.

The highway has many shortcomings, esthetic, economic, and social; it is often ugly, inefficient, and destructive to many communities. Yet even the most cluttered, the most garish and vulgar specimen has an immense potential. Moreover, the highway strip is developing a remarkable esthetic style of its own. Its lighting effects—not merely the neon signs but the indirect lighting of filling stations and drive-ins—are often extremely handsome; so are the bright, clear colors of the buildings and installations; so are the open spaces, even though they are not coordinated. It often seems that America is evolving a taste for a new kind of beauty: clean-cut geometric forms, primary colors, vast smooth surfaces and wide spaces uninterrupted by any detail, and bright lights. It is the beauty of newness, efficiency, and cleanliness, but to date, at least, it represents a thoroughly unsophisticated popular taste.

What is more significant is the social appeal of the highway strip, the chosen area of brief informal communication and social interaction. Drive through any medium-sized community in America after dark and you will at once see all the vitality is concentrated here—not along Main Street, and certainly not in the residential areas. This is where you will find the mixed public we so long to have in our central business district: teenagers, transients, people in search of amusement, doing business, alone and in group. And this is no ordinary street scene; this is specifically American.

The art and architecture of the strip is designed to attract. For all its flashiness it respects something like the human scale, it seeks to communicate and does so very successfully. Its topical frame of reference—the use of popular names, symbols, effects—even its very flimsiness and temporary quality make it congenial for informal temporary social intercourse, for it is a jumbled reminder of all current enthusiasms—atomic energy, space travel, Acapulco, folksinging, computers, Danish contemporary, health foods, hot-rod racing, and so on. And part of this congenial atmosphere is that it prescribes no traditional behavior; unlike the conventional park or even the public square, the strip allows almost complete freedom of conduct and dress.

The chief reason for the popularity of the strip, however, is that it is entirely adjusted to the automobile; it does not try to separate the automobile from its driver. It is characteristic of this generation to use not only the environment to create its identity but to use objects as well; and one of the most useful objects from this point of view is the automobile. It is adaptable, mobile, a means to gregariousness, and is common enough to be a recognizable means of communication in both senses of the word.

The adversary of the automobile is not the pedestrian as we may sometimes think, but the plot of land. Until about sixty years ago we believed in this country that possession of land and work on it created our identity. Everyone was supposed to have a homestead in order to be a good citizen and a well-rounded individual. To express the idea existentially, land was the object men could best use in their search for identity. The belief, of course, is very ancient and it is still held by many people. But it is doubtful if ever again in America it will have the same almost religious appeal. What has happened is that the land changed its status; it became a commodity, something which could be translated into money. We looked around for another usable object—and behold! the automobile appeared.

When we speak of the auto as a status symbol, we are speaking of new cars only; the average used car or jalopy is no status symbol of any sort. It is nevertheless an intimate part of its owner's identity. We all know the infinite variety of purposes the automobile serves—some very utilitarian, some social, and many of them psychological. The way we drive it, the way we work on it, the way we decorate it, all serve to identify us. A plausible theory could be developed that the greater the number of emotional problems there are among the young men in a family, the more cars you see in the front yard; working on a car is one of those tell-tale signs of emotional disturbances like a housewife's moving the furniture around; in both cases manipulating the environment serves as an outlet. Whatever the psychological role of the automobile, we do not like being separated from it for very long, particularly when we are not sure of ourselves. And the strip is a tacit recognition of this relationship.

There are good reasons for insisting on a separation between cars and people in certain parts of town, for the failure to separate them has caused the ruin of many places. We will not solve this problem, however, until we learn to see the car in another, more personal light; we have thought of it too much in terms of transportation. In Holland they have recognized the importance of the car in their new recreation areas; sociologists there have defined recreational needs in what can be called existential terms: "the need for sociability, the need to use one's own personal possessions [automobile], the need to collect experiences, and the need to run dangers."

The highway is merely one, though the most important, of these new centers of sociability. The others are the recreation area, the campground, and the motorsport track. All of these have at least one trait in common: the importance of the automobile. Should we not develop more of these meeting places and improve the ones which already exist? This is something the environmental designer can learn to do. Pedestrian malls and recreation and shopping areas which exclude the car are very desirable and can be made true works of art; but an even greater challenge is designing to integrate the automobile into certain types of gathering places. And the best place to study this sort of problem is along the highway strip.

Is this sort of intercourse the ultimate in human society? A landscape catering to our gregarious instincts is certainly better than one that isolates us; but are we not capable of something more productive and permanent? We are learning to redefine man as a social animal but we are not yet learning to define him as a political animal. We are evolving a social landscape as well, but this is not the ultimate in environmental design. A landscape allowed to expand to suit temporary needs leaves a great deal to be desired. Each of us feels the need for something permanent in the world surrounding us, just as we feel the need for a permanent identity for ourselves. This is not merely a matter of security or of objection to change. It is a matter of satisfying a fundamental human urge to be a part of an order which is more lasting than we are: a moral or ethical order which transcends our individual existence. The Romantic generations derived this kind of satisfaction from their feeling of oneness with nature. What do we have to take its place?

It is possible for the landscape to provide us with some symbols of permanent values. It is possible for it to provide us with landmarks to reassure us that we are not rootless individuals without identity or place, but are part of a larger scheme. The landscape can do much to reinforce our identity as political beings.

From *Landscapes* (University of Massachusetts Press, 1970).

Anthony, Georgia, Joseph, and Ruby Hernandez, South Williams Street SE, Albuquerque, Miguel Gandert

J. B. Jackson, cultural geographer, Anne Noggle

Rosa Wiley, seamstress, Anne Noggle

51

Two Street Scenes

Number one: Main Street, once planted with elms and possessing broad sidewalks, has been entirely transformed. First one row of trees was chopped down, then the other, and finally the sidewalks were reduced by half. Now the street accommodates six lanes of traffic instead of three. Whatever was left of the street's original character has been destroyed by two recent municipal ordinances: one forbids parking during business hours, the other makes it a one-way street. Another street, parallel to Main, has been made one-way in the opposite direction.

The result, technologically speaking, is most impressive. It is true that the property owners and merchants along Main Street don't like it and that the public is a little uneasy without knowing why; but traffic experts and safety engineers and trucking executives and city officials come from far and wide to see how Main Street has been improved.

A tide of buses and trucks and passenger cars, usually five abreast, surges through the heart of the city at 20 to 25 MPH, eight hours a day. The authorities hope to increase this speed by one means or another. Meanwhile they have installed clusters of overhead traffic lights, equipped with gongs, at every intersection. The sidewalk corners have been chained off to prevent pedestrians from crossing diagonally. Jaywalkers are handed summonses by the police and in addition are given a brief memorized sermon on the hazards of crossing against the lights. Once a year the Junior Chamber of Commerce, to show its zeal for the public good, hires a comedian-acrobat to put on a show at high noon at the intersection of Main and First streets. The public pauses to watch the clown dodge in and out among the moving cars, vault over the hoods, collapse on the bumpers and so on—a good half hour of laughs and chills. The crowd disperses, temporarily scornful of any pedestrian who would interfere with the flow of traffic by jaywalking.

When the lights change there is a clanging of bells, and the occasional sound of a policeman's whistle; cars which have been delayed a second in their getaway make a furious bleating. Then the cataract resumes. Sharp-eyed policemen watch the flow, either from the curb or on motorcycles, and usually a police car with a two-way radio and a traffic expert on the front seat cruises downstream to make sure that nothing occurs to interrupt or slow down the steady flow of vehicles. It is all extremely well managed.

How fares it with the pedestrian on Main Street? An unusual question. If he stays to the right of the sidewalk, conforms to the average rate of progress, runs when the lights are about to change; if he does not loiter or turn around or try to walk abreast of someone else; generally speaking, if he behaves like an automaton he will get along sufficiently well. Actually he has learned not to expect any pleasure from walking down Main Street; he is not likely to do more than proceed straight ahead until he reaches his destination. There are few distractions left in this part of town, though there used to be plenty. The trees are gone, the benches where there were street-car stops are gone. City ordinances, widely approved at the time, have forbidden any beggars or musicians or vendors or shoeshine boys or pushcarts from appearing in the downtown area. All commercial displays must be behind glass and even window displays must not be of a nature to attract crowds and thus slow up traffic. For some reason the merchants seek to attract the attention of the passing motorist and not that of the passing pedestrian; so almost all the signs are above the street level.

During work hours street and sidewalk are crowded; after work hours they are all but empty. A few cars hurtle down the deserted traffic-way with its succession of blinking yellow lights at the intersections. A few pedestrians, headed for a show or a restaurant, park their car and hurry to a side street. The store windows are dark. The only color and gaiety comes from the electric and neon lights halfway up the facades. Main Street, within the memory of man, was once the center of the city. Transformed and streamlined to satisfy special interests, it has now destroyed most of the city's communal outdoor life, and frightened away the remainder.

Scene number two: This Main Street, far older and far narrower than the other, is always hopelessly congested. It always has been during its more than three centuries of existence, and it always will be. It and the nearby square constitute the very heart of the town and its corporate life. Main Street leads nowhere; it merely exists.

At nine A.M. there is a wedding in the cathedral. A hooting procession of some ten cars, all festooned with ribbons and streamers, comes down Main Street, paying no attention to traffic lights, and goes twice around the square, making as much noise and being as conspicuously happy as possible. Everyone pauses to watch, and finds some comment to make. Traffic may have been temporarily paralyzed, but the stock of public pleasure and wisdom has been greatly increased. At 11 A.M. there is another wedding with precisely the same effect.

By late morning, the rodeo stages a celebration in the form of a parade twice the length of Main Street and once around the square. Twenty-five cars, six trucks with bands or floats and adorned with aggressive slogans alternate with groups of cheering and singing students. The parade passes at 10 MPH; the air reeks of scorched brake linings and exhaust. An even younger public watches enviously from the sidewalk. While this is going on all traffic comes to a dead stop. Drivers wait with a greater or lesser degree of patience and goodwill, but they wait, and whether they relish it or not for the time being they are involved in the life of the community.

Throughout the day (and much of the night) there are groups of idlers on every corner crossing whenever and wherever they please to pass the time of day with friends loitering on another corner. There is a fraudulent beggar or two, Indians selling jewelry; wife and child squat on the nearby sidewalk and placidly consume a picnic lunch. There are cars stopping and backing up to greet a passerby.

Pedestrians and motorists are on the most cordial terms. On occasion the street is roped off after dark for dancing or a band concert.

Far from becoming subdued when the work day is done, Main Street and the square used to be at their liveliest from five o'clock on, and what's more, the life was chiefly pedestrian.

Now the first of these scenes is in almost any small American city which has the fortune (or misfortune) to be situated on an important freight highway and to possess a city council that likes to try to solve traffic problems for the exclusive benefit of the motorist. The second happens to be in Santa Fe, New Mexico. But the essential contrast between the two kinds of street is not that between industrial and nonindustrial communities or even that between coherent and incoherent city plans. It is the contrast between those communities which with the best of intentions have allowed their streets to be used and planned almost exclusively for heavy and rapid through traffic, and a community where the streets are still common property, still part of the living space of every citizen. It is not too much to say that there is pageantry of a sort in the streets out here, whereas there is none in the streets of the average American city of today.

Many factors have helped preserve this kind of communal life in Santa Fe. The city fathers have had nothing to do with it, and there is a large and vociferous element that is ashamed of the town's informality. But we are lucky in possessing a population that is gregarious and at the same time hostile to police regulation, and that remains loyal to a long-established tradition of group pleasures. Yet something of this color and vitality could be introduced to many other American cities; it is merely a matter of establishing (or reestablishing) the principle that streets are not intended solely for motor traffic but were made for any and every kind of outdoor group activity, from children's games to funeral processions and endless loitering in the sun. All civic architecture is essentially nothing but an appropriate background for this life; and city planning is chiefly justified when it helps preserve and foster informal communal activities.

As far as Santa Fe is concerned, we can be sure that the population will never entirely abandon even the widest and straightest of streets to motor traffic. There will always be some carefree jaywalker to cross in front of you without warning: a teenage motorcyclist to show off for the drugstore crowd, a dog-fight, or a wedding. Always, in short, a reminder that the motorist does not own the streets but merely shares them with others.

Landscape 3, no. 3 (Spring 1954): 4–5.

125 West Water Street, Santa Fe, February 1982, Richard Wilder

125 West Water Street, Santa Fe, February 1983, Richard Wilder

Goodbye to Evolution

Of all the reasons for preserving a fragment of the landscape—picturesque farm valley, village with fields and meadows, pastoral view—the esthetic is surely the poorest one. And the fact that many still think it the best reason of all derives from a point of view which should be discarded as fast as possible.

Specifically, it derives from the theory that human landscapes are subject to a gradual and predictable process of evolution. Countless textbooks and museum dioramas have explained the various stages a landscape goes through—depending of course on the natural environment: first the primeval forest, then the pioneer with his ax or his girdling technique, then the first fields of corn or wheat; then more and more houses and finally something like a village rising in the midst of the now pretty completely humanized landscape, with a crude kind of dam somewhere in the picture. Patrick Geddes, in his *Cities in Evolution* (a book most planners are familiar with) traces the evolution well into the industrial age, with villages becoming manufacturing or trading centers, then becoming larger and larger cities—*connurbations* was his word for them—and then the landscape of the future.

Implicit in most of these schemes was the assumption that there existed what ecologists call a climax form of the human landscape: a form in which changes were relatively stabilized and where natural resources were in balance with local demand; a kind of utopia. Sometimes this climax form of the human landscape was identified with a self-contained rural society, like the Mennonites or the Pueblo Indians; sometimes it was located in the future, a goal toward which we were all inevitably (if unconsciously) working. It was generally agreed, in any case, that we knew what the ideal landscape was; and that insofar as some existing landscapes *looked* ideal, *i.e.*, were picturesque and stable, they certainly ought to be preserved for posterity.

If geographers and historians and anthropologists are sure that this is the way human landscapes evolved in the past—in an orderly, gradual, inevitable sequence—then the least we can do is believe them, for they have put a good deal of work into elaborating the theory. But we need only look around us to see that the law no longer holds true and that the human landscape is changing in quite a different manner. Its changes are entirely unpredictable, and they often bypass one or more stages in the evolutionary process. A midwestern farm, planted to corn, becomes, in the course of a few months, a residential community of 10,000 inhabitants with a few light industries. An alpine slope, hitherto occupied by grazing cows, suddenly sprouts a dozen high-rise apartment houses. A desert valley is transformed into an area of intensive truck farming, and the picturesque New England village finds itself at the bottom of an immense reservoir, with its hillside fields planted to conifers.

All such landscape changes can easily be explained in social and economic terms, of course; there is nothing mysterious about them. But there is nothing remotely evolutionary or ecological about them, either. They are what the avant-garde calls "happenings"—geographical happenings. The point is, the old established theory of landscape formation has to be scrapped as far as the present and the predictable future are concerned. Instead of evolving, working toward a climax, the human landscape is changing by a series of violent and unpredictable mutations, and no one is foolhardy enough to pretend to foresee what it will look like a generation hence.

Now it is obvious that many of these mutations are for the worse in almost every sense; but it is equally obvious that in our modern world the notion of a climax form for the human landscape, or any kind of teleological thinking on the subject, is very much out of place and this means— does it not?—that we have got to find new criteria for the worth of a human landscape, existing or projected. Its place on the evolutionary ladder won't do, neither will its esthetic qualities or its capacity for making money, though these two beliefs are very popular at present. As Chester Beaty says,

Those to whom the pattern appears "for worse" must do more than simply decry a

trend already well established . . . planning will be done, based upon whatever measures of "betterment" are available. The American penchant for big, bigger, biggest is somehow going to have to be translated into language understood and respected by both the profit-maximizers and the "humanists." The primary responsibility . . . rests with the latter.

Sooner or later every planner, every landscape architect, every conservationist will have to acknowledge this challenge. It is not a comfortable one; it leaves us no certainties to depend on, no geographical or ecological laws to help us out: merely an obligation to rethink what a landscape is worth to the person who inhabits it.

We can get nearer to an answer by abandoning the spectator stance and seeking to identify ourselves and our desires with the landscape, by asking ourselves how any man would fare who had to live in it. What chances (for instance) does the landscape offer for making a living? What chances does it offer for freedom of choice of action? What chances for meaningful relationships with other men and with the landscape itself? What chances for individual fulfillment and for social change? Judged in these terms, many industrialized and suburban landscapes would be found wanting; but so would many picturesque rural landscapes as well.

We are, to be sure, not likely to adopt these standards as long as we prefer simply to think of the landscape as something to look at, a spectacle conducive to day-dreaming. And, if it were really nothing but that, it would be right for us to preserve it, design it, transform it according to a popular taste for the picturesque. If we did that, America would be a far more beautiful country than it is. But we are *not* spectators; the human landscape is *not*

a work of art. It is the temporary product of much sweat and hardship and earnest thought; we should never look at it without remembering that, and we should never tinker with the landscape without thinking of those who live in the midst of it—whether in a trailer in an oil field or in a city tenement. What the spectator wants or does not want is of small account.

For better or worse, we have become an uncertain, unpredictable, mobile race of men. If the landscape is to be truly human it ought to reflect the kind of people we are. It would be nice to have it beautiful, but it *must* be fluid and capable of sudden change, no matter how it may have evolved in the past.

Landscape 13, no. 2 (Winter 1963–64): 1–2.

College Well and Reservoir, Albuquerque, Thomas F. Barrow

Franciscan Reservoir, Albuquerque, Thomas F. Barrow

East Mesa Construction, Las Cruces, Richard Wickstrom

El Pueblo, West Mesa Subdivision, Las Cruces, Richard Wickstrom

Salt Beds, near Loving, Mary Peck

Chihuahua
as we might have been

There have not been many frontiers like this one, I imagine. An abstraction, a Euclidean line drawn across the desert, has created two distinct human landscapes where there was only one before. Much of the frontier is river, and rivers are meant to bring men together, not to keep them apart. The rest of it is a straight scientific line inscribed in sand, no more related to the terrain, no more part of the view than are those groups of letters which maps show to the north and south of it: Chihuahua and Texas and New Mexico.

Line and river, idea and unifying force, they have been made to divide an entity which the earth created and men accepted for some three hundred years—the Spanish Southwest. Speaking in terms of a relatively lengthy past and its physical setting, New Mexico and that western wedge of Texas and Chihuahua all belong to the same high mountainous semiarid region that was once called New Biscay. Or should I say that New Mexico and a fragment of Texas are the northward extensions of Chihuahua? Politically they certainly were. All three areas were not only discovered, explored, and taken possession of in the same northwestward movement of the Spaniards out of Mexico, but were eventually settled by the same

breed of colonists: miners and hunters and ranchmen. And Santa Barbara, the southernmost (and the oldest) town in Chihuahua to this day, likes to think of Santa Fe far to the north as a sort of daughter city. The Romeros, Trujillos, Martinezes that abound in both places must then be cousins, I suppose, many miles and generations removed. One language, one law, one kind of economy—a predatory one—and one prevailing set of manners and values—all these things the line has destroyed.

But it is of course the physical make-up of this old Southwest that gives it its fundamental unity, and a whole network of Euclidean lines could not destroy that. Topography, climate, vegetation, the very quality of the sunlight and distance and the solitude are the same north of the border and south. Though it may change its name from Rio Grande to Rio Bravo, its course from due south to southeast, the one great river with its tributaries dominates the region, just as its articulations, its valleys and passes have always determined the location of roads and farms and villages. As for mountains, who can say in the Southwest what range or system any of them belongs to? Only the Sangre de Cristos, we are told, are part of the Rockies; all the others have origins of their own. Still, I think that most of them, aside from their differences of altitude and bulk, share a certain local southwestern character and are unlike mountains elsewhere. They trend for the most part north and south, and are isolated from one another by great wide valleys and plains. They leap up out of the range or desert like dark red, spiney-backed monsters at play in the sea, and sink abruptly. Their steep flanks are barren except for cascades of sand and gravel and rock, cascades which seem only now to have stopped streaming, as if yesterday the mass had suddenly heaved out of the flatness. No horizon to the south but is alive with extravagant peaks: dark orange, dark blue, pale blue and pink and violet, the color of clinkers. And yet for all their omnipresence the mountains here and in Chihuahua are almost totally useless, producing no gold, no rain, no permanent streams, no forests, and scarcely any pasture. They are background, essential for esthetic purposes, dignifying or dwarfing the activities of man, whichever you prefer.

Mountains are the same, weather is the same; a little dryer to the south, a little hotter, but not without bleak winds to whip across the treeless expanses. Vegetation likewise much the same. Chamisa is absent and so are piñon trees, but their places are taken by creosote and mesquite. After one of the rare showers in the Chihuahua desert the dampened leaves of the creosote make the air smell of witch-hazel just as it does in southern New Mexico. And while the moisture lasts, the short, sparse grass becomes green, wildflowers cover the hollows of the range with sheets of yellow and silver, and there is a profusion of meadowlarks singing. The same limpid air, the same overpowering sun. And the same intense blue sky, immaculate day after day except for one long, thin cloud the tone of aluminum.

So they were made to be one and the same, Chihuahua and west Texas and New Mexico, and they were thought of as one by the people who lived north and south—until the line was drawn. Now there are two Southwests, or rather a Mexican Northwest and our own Southwest, related but no longer identical. For what has happened is not merely that a homogeneous region has been divided between two nations—that could always be undone—but that two distinct human landscapes, each the expression of a different kind of society, have been created; and such a distinction is likely to last forever.

Our own we know, or think we know. But what is the most marked characteristic of the human landscape immediately to the south of us? To the North American traveler, in search of that color and variety usually associated with Mexico, Chihuahua is bitterly disappointing, and its most striking feature, exhilarating at first, then depressing, is its emptiness. Our own Southwest has its lonely prospects, but none so lonely, I should think, as those in Chihuahua. Vast enough to contain the history and monuments of a whole race, its wide valleys seem to be as devoid of humanity as was the world on the eve of the sixth day. No matter where you look in New Mexico or west Texas—provided the view is of normal extent—you are likely to see some evidence of man's work: a far-off ranch house with a windmill, a wire fence, a telephone or light pole, a roadside store, sometimes the green of a patch of irrigated land down in a wash. In Chihuahua there is little of the sort; nothing for the twenty or thirty or forty miles at a stretch to reassure you that men have lived here and probably live here still. The miles go by, the mountains slowly revolve out of sight and new ones appear; and at last you see a file of mottle-faced, long-limbed, wild-eyed cows, of the sort we still derisively call Chihuahuas, wandering across the range. Strictly speaking even these are not evidence of human occupancy of the landscape, though they would certainly be elsewhere greener and better watered were it not for human interference.

There are towns and even cities to the south, quite true; and whole countrysides where the soil is cultivated with an intensity we scarcely know; but these are merely interruptions of the prevailing solitude; they do not constitute a continuous pattern and do little to alter that first impression. It happens to be a very correct impression, I believe. It is another and more immediate way of sensing that the human landscape is only feebly developed. I do not merely mean that the population is small for so large an area; it is, though it is actually more dense than that of New Mexico; nor that there is anything primitive about the social setup in Chihuahua. On the contrary. But whatever the society, it has only sketched the broad outline of its pattern on the face of the earth. It has built towns and cities in considerable number, but it has only begun to formulate its own characteristic countryside. Our own Southwest, on the other hand, has been almost completely transformed in the image of our own way of life. It is as if two different sets of laws, two distinct psychologies, were at work.

Now the explanation for this underdevelopment, or at least one explanation, is not hard to discover. It is undoubtedly true that much of Chihuahua is rangeland, if not worse, and could at best support a very small number of ranchers. But the thing is, during most of the four centuries since the arrival of the Spaniards it has supported no one at all. The Apache and Comanche raids, beginning as soon as those tribes had acquired horses from the invaders, made the region an unhealthy one not only for would-be settlers but for military and commercial traffic passing through to New Mexico in the north. Garrisons were established at strategic points, especially in the open country where the Apaches preferred to operate, and expeditions against the Indians were almost constant. With

little success; toward the middle of the eighteenth century, security, at least for travelers, was achieved, but then the Jesuit missionaries in the mountains to the west were withdrawn on orders from Spain, and Spanish authority was weakened as a result. The Apaches once more became aggressive, and when Mexico declared its independence of the mother country the greatest concern of Chihuahua was not the drawing up of a suitably republican state constitution, but how to defend itself against the Indian raids. These in fact had become so effective that the settlers in the open country had retreated altogether to the garrison towns or to the mountains or to the larger centers like Chihuahua city and Parral. The chronicles of these communities makes for sorry reading: settled in the seventeenth or eighteenth centuries and given a resounding name, abandoned a few decades later (and often once again) because of the depredations of the Indians, the "Naturales."

Such a state of affairs was more or less paralleled in our own part of the continent, but here it never resulted in the complete depopulation of a desirable stretch of land, nor did it ever last for long. In Chihuahua it lasted until about the middle of the 1880s. It was only then that the vast cattle country in the northern and eastern part of the state was finally safe for settlement. And again a political situation intervened. If ranching had for long been delayed by the inability of the government to maintain order, ranching on a prosperous basis was handicapped under the Diaz regime by a government policy of encouraging monster cattle empires. The largest ranch in Chihuahua (and incidentally in all of Mexico) contained no less than six and a half million acres—about the size of Belgium. There were until not many years ago five other ranches with more than a million acres apiece, and altogether more than a third of the entire state, which is not much smaller than Arizona, was owned by seventeen men. Much of this land was, to be sure, of very limited

Near Maes, Mary Peck

worth, but some of it was extremely valuable. A ranch of almost a million acres west of Chihuahua city, once the property of a family who ran a few thousand head of cattle on it and eventually went bankrupt, now supports ten thousand prosperous Mennonite farmers, with room for many more.

I see no reason, I confess, why a large ranch cannot exploit the land just as well as a medium size or small one. But in practice these enormous holdings were totally inefficient. At a time when the Anglo-Saxon world was beginning to discover the romance of ranching in the Wild West, and when British and American capital was pouring into the cattle industry, the ranchers of northern Mexico had an altogether different point of view. Disdaining to live in the primitive solitude of their estates, they built palaces in town and furnished them with boatloads of finery from Italy and France. Their lavish spending was the admiration of Europe, but they begrudged money for nails, and so the ranch buildings were held together with rawhide. One of these ranches is said to have branded 140,000 steers in one year. But nevertheless no equipment was bought for farming, no wells were drilled, no good stock was ever bred, and no range conservation even of the most rudimentary sort was dreamed of. Nor were any fences to divide the range into pastures ever erected, though stone walls, miles in extent and still a conspicuous feature of the otherwise bleak landscape, were sometimes built. The enforced self-sufficiency of these ranches, to say nothing of the low scale of pay of the workers, discouraged the growth of any rural retail centers in the neighborhood. All in all, it would be hard to conceive of a more benighted economy than this, or a more picturesque one. The florid mansions and the legends of high living are only part of its legacy, however. Rangeland remote from the natural waterholes is still largely untouched, villages are still practically nonexistent, and

except for the overgrazed areas near water and the tumbled remains of those massive walls, the whole countryside is today much as it must have been four hundred years ago.

Would efficiency have overtaken these holdings in time? Quite possibly. The American market for beef has always been the largest one for Chihuahua, and in the course of organizing to exploit it, the landowners in spite of themselves might have incidentally created a more articulate landscape—retail villages, small farms, roads and windbreaks and water tanks and small pastures. In any case, such was the development in the United States. But a generation ago the era of large ranches in northern Mexico came to an end—not, as we are fond of supposing in parallel cases, because they were uneconomical or obsolete, but because of a revolution. The revolutionary wars started in the first decade of the century and lasted until well after 1920, causing almost as much damage of every description as did the far better known First World War in Europe. The large ranches were naturally objects of special attention from the revolutionists, but the whole region, indeed the whole nation, suffered to a degree that we in this country have never appreciated. Before the revolution Chihuahua had two and a half million head of cattle; twenty years later it had little more than a quarter of that amount. The Mexican northwest has always been the land of horsemen; Chihuahua had 730,000 horses before the revolution and lost four-fifths of them. Nor was this the result of any shift in the economy; it was entirely the work of a prolonged and ruinous war which leveled villages, destroyed railroads, uprooted the population, and brought every agricultural enterprise to a standstill.

Actually it was not so much the violent aspect of the revolution that did away with the big ranches as it was the social revolution which came after; and the first real change in the human landscape—a change more evident on paper than in the scenery itself, but still a change—came when the large holdings were divided up for the benefit of the less prosperous. Socially and economically speaking the Land Reform Laws were epochal, I have no doubt, but their total effect on the pattern of settlement has been far less marked than one might suppose. For unhappily it is not enough to give a man a few thousand acres of land; he needs not only cattle, but money for wells and fences and corrals and feed, and the average rancher south of the Rio Grande has never had money or credit of that kind. And then finally two more factors (not political this time) have militated against a full development of the rural areas: the hoof-and-mouth disease and the local drought. The disease never prevailed in Chihuahua, but the United States embargo on Mexican meat nevertheless killed the best outlet for beef. The prolonged drought, still not everywhere broken, affected the grass on the range less than it affected the supply of surface water; but the results were the same. As for the underground water supply, it is largely intact, because who has the money to drill wells and put in windmills and tanks? Plaintive and frequent requests have been made to the government, but to no avail. The chief concern at the moment is not the rancher and his plight—a perennial topic—but the small farmers, the colonists on the large and costly irrigation projects.

So the ranchers, obliged to shift for themselves, have been able to do little or nothing. The countryside, however equitably subdivided, remains much as it has always been, and the development of a full-fledged pattern of settlement remains a very nebulous prospect.

Here then is an environment in every important respect like our own rangeland—in climate, vegetation, water supply, topography—where nevertheless a totally different kind of human landscape prevails. And how are we to account for this dissimilarity? Chiefly, I think, by considering some of those imponderable factors which go to make every landscape what it is, and of these the psychological is not the least influential. There has in fact evolved to the south of us a landscape of towns and cities, a surprisingly rich and numerous constellation of communities located as it were in a void. Chihuahua has more towns of over ten thousand inhabitants than New Mexico and Arizona, and they are not sleepy market towns, either. That is one reason why they are not visited by tourists; they are almost completely lacking in beauty and charm. The air does not smell of cinnamon and chocolate and lime, no wild birds call out in the laurel trees of the plaza, and there is little of the public gaiety of a more genial climate. The antiquities of Chihuahua are neither numerous nor impressive (though they would loom large in New Mexico or Arizona), and they are usually hidden in the welter of neon signs and telegraph poles and dwarf skyscrapers and neo-Aztec architecture of the business streets. The smaller towns are a gridiron of low houses bordering dusty and windswept streets, streets too broad and too long, and with the harsh mountains or the desert at the end of all of them, no matter what their length. You begin to suspect in these drab surroundings that Texas cannot be very far away, and that Yankee Imperialism is doing its fell work in even the remotest places.

But actually these towns are all bona fide Chihuahuan, which is to say they have a character very much of their own: detached from the countryside, self-contained, and within limits remarkably urban. Chihuahua city, neither particularly rich nor blessed with many monuments, has nevertheless a dignity and a scale that would put many North American cities to shame. What should not be forgotten is that these towns were none of them originally rural marketplaces; they are all artificial and carefully designed communities which have not yet attained their full metropolitan growth and perhaps never will.

There are several very good reasons for this concentration in towns and for the urban character of the towns themselves. The largest and oldest settlements in Chihuahua are after all mining centers, possessing many features of cities far larger and more industrialized than they: a small class of very rich men, a large proletariat, and little if any traditional connection with the nearby farmers and ranchers. All past efforts to expand into the open country have been roughly discouraged, and finally a large community in the midst of semidesert country has to be self-sufficient if it is to survive.

But still, I cannot believe that such explanations, practical though they are, really account for the concentration in towns; I cannot believe that there is not some national or racial trait also at work: in brief, a partiality for city life. The kind of architecture a group prefers—when it has any choice in the matter—can be very revealing of the group's temperament. The poor in Chihuahua, even in the large cities, build as best they can, which is to say they build as the farmers do: out of adobe. But the more prosperous citizens like their houses to be more elegant, and so in northern Mexico the rural architectural tradition is one of the first things to be discarded when social respectability arrives. As for the very rich, the ranchers or mine owners or officeholders or generals, their houses are likely to repudiate every local tradition of plan and material and ornamentation. Not deliberately, I suppose, but nonetheless completely. In the old days of Porfirism, as they call the regime of Diaz, the ideal home seems to have been something ornate, formal, and reminiscent of a European social order—Paris or Madrid at two removes. What is the ideal now? Something not easy to define, but easy enough to recognize: a blend of Hollywood and Tel-Aviv and Frank Lloyd Wright; wrought iron and plate glass and tapestry brick and bougainvillea and Kubla Khan's pleasure dome, conspicuously, not to say defiantly located in the midst of an English lawn. If as someone once incautiously remarked, architecture is frozen music, this is Spike Jones straight from the deep freeze. But more than that, it is a very definite rejection of the whole rural background.

It may be objected that Chihuahua has no rural tradition except of having to flee from the Apaches, and that unlike other parts of Mexico (and New Mexico) it never had a sedentary Indian population to establish an indigenous architectural style. True; but what it *does* possess is a vast amount of that kind of building which we in the Southwest call the Spanish Pueblo style. Without going into the touchy problem of where this style originated, I think most will agree that Chihuahua, however scantily populated, has an infinitely greater number and variety of those squat adobe constructions than we in the Southwest ever had. But here is where one of those imponderables comes in: Chihuahua, the rich and official Chihuahua, the Chihuahua which builds churches and public buildings and hundred-thousand-dollar residences, will have none of this adobe style. It wants something more elaborate, even if synthetic. It wants an architecture which reflects what may be called the southwestern dream, a dream which was (and in Mexico still is) compounded of wealth based on mining and ranching, Spanish background, and the amenities of city life: a culture which has unconsciously retained the original dual meaning of urbanity.

As to what the racial origins of the population of Chihuahua are I have no idea. They may well be all of them descendants of the Spanish conquistadores, and again they may be a mixture of every Indian group in Mexico. But what matters is how they think and act, and to me one of the charms of northern Mexico is that its people think not as Indians but as Latins. More than a century ago Humboldt was much impressed by the vigor and clarity of thought among a group which at that time was still a rough pioneer community for the rest of Mexico, and he predicted that this northern region—in which I suppose he meant to include Arizona and New Mexico, for he wrote before the annexation—would in time be distinguished for its mathematicians and scientists. Was it Los Alamos that he foresaw? Latin rationalism, however, has assumed a different form; a taste for politics and political theory, and it is that taste which has to a surprising extent formed the human landscape. *If* the missionaries had not been withdrawn in the eighteenth century there would have been a peaceful Indian population to contribute to the welfare of the country; *if* the Apache had been prevented by a strong government from going on the warpath in the nineteenth century there would have been more ranches, more farms, more country villages. *If* there had been no revolution in the early decades of this century there would have been a more even distribution of the population. And if in the past political events have so determined the demographic aspects of the world, or at least of Chihuahua, why can they not continue to do so in the future? Divide the estates by law, build highways and new towns and irrigation projects according to a plan, create a new party to execute the plan, and the political process goes on with unabated vigor. And no doubt it will. Much Mexican political activity must forever bewilder the foreigner, but some of it becomes intelligible, I find, when it is understood that to the south of the Rio Grande the world of man is thought of as created in the likeness of a social theory and not, as with us, in the likeness of

an economic force. The elaborate geometrical layout of every modern Mexican community—gridiron or hexagon or concentric figures—the policy of naming streets after political abstractions when they are not numbered—and even sometimes when they are—and of renaming old towns after contemporary political heroes, are merely the most obvious manifestations of a determination to impose design and political direction on an unreasoning world. Gentes de Razon versus Naturales; and when the Naturales vanish than versus nature itself.

And this theoretical conquest of the region has already been accomplished. On paper, and in the conviction of its citizens, the Mexican earth, amorphous as much of it must seem to us, is divided and subdivided a dozen different ways, classified and surveyed. In this manner even the uninhabited desert has been tamed. The steepest hill, the poorest village in Chihuahua can always somehow be benefited by an application of geometry and politics.

Something of the same belief persists among the Spanish population of New Mexico and Arizona. It would do us no harm, I think, if we had more of it, if more of the Latin faith in reason rather than in power had spread northward into our country before the line was drawn. But it was drawn a hundred years ago, and now there are two nations, two landscapes, two ways of looking at the world and of living in it. In time the Southwest will lose its identity, but the aspects of it that we value and try to keep alive hark back to that large undivided region; it is Chihuahua which represents the original even now. What is alike between New Mexico and the old is the heritage of Chihuahua. Chihuahua is what we once were: a sunstruck landscape full of bright plans for the future.

Landscape 1, no. 1 (Spring 1951): 16–23.

Lake Bed, Palo Blanco, Mary Peck

Way down, south of Animas, close to Mexico (Route 338), Bernard Plossu

76

Sunset and dust, rodeo south of Animas (southern New Mexico), Bernard Plossu

Bathers, First Plaza, Albuquerque, Miguel Gandert

Landscape as Theater

When we speak of the "scenes of our childhood," or borrow Pope's phrase and refer to the world as "this scene of man," we are using the word *scene* in what seems a literal sense: as meaning location, the place where something happens. It rarely occurs to us that we have in fact borrowed a word from the theater to use as a metaphor. Yet originally *scene* meant stage, as it still does in French, and when it first became common in everyday speech it still suggested its origin: the world (we were implying) was a theater, and we were at once actors and audience.

The notion that a bond exists between people and the world they inhabit is fundamental to our understanding of life, and the bond has usually been seen as that between parents and children. The metaphor drawn from the theater seems to have become popular at a comparatively late date, no earlier than the sixteenth century. Its formulation implies three things: the development of the theatrical production as a formal art with its own rules and conventions and its own environment; a widespread belief that the relationship between people and their surroundings could be so expertly controlled and designed as to make the comparison appropriate; and, most important of all, the metaphor implies people's ability to see themselves as occupying the center of the stage.

It was logical that the theater arts as we know them should have evolved first in Italy in the early sixteenth century, for it was there that the art (or science) of perspective arose—the art, that is to say, of defining or depicting a body in terms of the space it occupies. The first stage sets were the work of Italian artists and architects and technicians, and it was in Italy that we find the first stage, the first area defined in terms of the relation between actors and audience, and in fact the first building designed exclusively for theatrical productions. For more than a century the standard theater was known as the Italian-style theater; the term meant not only the building itself, but stage, scenery, the whole illusion of space achieved by the skillful use of light and color and form: the space of a make-believe world which revolved around the presence of actors.

It was surely no accident that at much the same period artists began to paint pictures of landscapes. It was Albrecht Dürer who, after his return from Italy, first sketched from life some of the villages he traveled through. The painters of northern Europe differed from those of Italy in their interest in the everyday aspect of the landscape; they often chose as their subject village celebrations or glimpses of peasants at work in the fields, whereas the Italian painters preferred to use the rustic landscape as a somewhat remote background for more formal subjects inspired by myth or philosophy. But in both cases landscape was an element in the composition, serving to locate or define the human action. The artist modified or even restructured the background scenery in order to produce a harmony between the world of man and the world of nature.

The last decades of the sixteenth century and the first decades of the seventeenth witnessed the development of still another form of landscape depiction: the rise of descriptive geography. Geography had previously been little more than a branch of cosmography—the study of the earth as a heavenly body. The growing interest in Classical literature encouraged the investigation and description of places mentioned in Greek and Latin texts, and a renewed study of Classical writers on geography. What first evolved was therefore a kind of historical geography. But the impact of the reports of explorers of the New World and of Asia soon expanded the field. Travelers, merchants, missionaries all contributed to a wider and more accurate knowledge of the earth's surface and at the same time supplemented or corrected Classical accounts. An abundant literature of topographical description, enriched by maps and illustrations of cities and landscapes and exotic costumes, was the outcome of this first wave of geographical inquiry.

It was characteristic of those early productions that they emphasized the human or political aspects of the world: boundaries, territorial divisions, language, towns, and cities. Only insofar as they served as frontiers were rivers and mountains mentioned. All of them dwelt on

history, military or dynastic; but history as then conceived included legends and myths. The writings of Mandeville and Münster and of many of the early travelers in the New World contained not only much valuable information about little-known regions but also a large element of the fabulous, and generalizations based on hearsay. In the minds of the writers the distinction between fact and fancy was neither clear nor important. Scientific accuracy was not the aim of the descriptive geographers: they sought to make the world visible and to inspire wonder.

From the point of view of the student of landscapes and their evolution, the sixteenth and seventeenth centuries represent one of the most important periods in our Western history. It was then that men first undertook to impose order and design on their surroundings not merely to survive but to produce a kind of beauty glorifying and making visible a particular relationship among men, and between men and nature. There was scarcely a discipline that did not contribute to the undertaking. The artist was the first to see and depict men and women, not as isolated figures but as dominating their environment. It was the cartographer who delineated territories, revealing their form and relating them one to another. It was the geographer who undertook to describe the world and the bond between people and the land they occupied. Always the emphasis was on the visual; the world and everything in it was a source of delight, and all that could be seen and understood by vision was worthy of study.

In those times a word much used in the titles of books of travel and description was *theater*. A popular textbook was called the *Theater of Geography*, a book of pictures was called the *Theater of Cities*. There were books called the *Theater of Agriculture*, the *Theater of the Garden*, the *Theater of the World*. The word of course emphasized the visual, the spectacular aspect of the environment, but it also suggested a spectacle in the sense of a dramatic production with a well-defined space, an organization of place and time, and coherent action.

Theater was thus a useful and appropriate metaphor, but more than that, it gave the ultimate three-dimensional form to all the chorographic, esthetic, and philosophical theories redefining men and the world. In retrospect it is clear why the drama should have been the dominant art form of an age concerned with place and visibility and the Classical image of humanity. It is clear why the theater developed new techniques of staging precisely when artists and cartographers and geographers were beginning to describe the suface of the earth. Lope de Vega wrote the *Great Theater of the World*; Shakespeare, among others, reminded us that all the world was a stage. It was in theatrical terms, therefore, that man's place could be interpreted as a work of art, his identity best established.

It is tempting to assume that this recognition of the environment and its role in establishing human identity signified a scientific interest in nature. But this does not seem to have been the case. Beautiful though the world of nature might be, it was nevertheless seen essentially as background, the realm of myth and magic. The scenery which artists, architects, engineers created on the sixteenth-century stage was far from realistic. It consisted of the illusion of great distances, vertical as well as horizontal, of architecture on a monumental scale, of supernatural light and movement. Even the plays of Shakespeare, though modestly produced as compared to Italian and French plays, were performed in an atmosphere of magic. Many unholy sound effects accompanied the action: bells, cannon, thunder, birdsong. The wind blew, the sea crashed, echoes resounded. Music was closely coordinated with the development of the drama and underscored the lyrical or passionate episodes. On the continent, stage designers produced impressive cloud effects with thunder and lightning and the illusion of mountains and stormy seas suddenly appearing or vanishing, or parting to reveal an elaborately costumed ballet. Pagan divinities descended from the sky, cities were consumed by fire, destroyed by earthquakes. In a Spanish production of the sixteenth century, God Himself was shown, surrounded by saints and hovering angels. In a play given in Rome and staged by the architect Bernini, the entire stage was suddenly flooded.

The purpose of these elaborate illusions was to amaze and delight a public eager for visual pleasures, for the sensation of space, and to entertain those who were perhaps not able to follow the drama itself. In the early days of the new theater many conventions, carried over from court or church ceremonies, effectively destroyed any feeling of realism. Writing and acting were still inexpert. The left side of the stage was considered the most prestigious location and actors sought to stand there, regardless of the action of the play. When not reciting their lines, they frequently greeted friends in the audience, and, in fact, favored members of the audience came and sat on the stage, commenting loudly on the performance and interfering with the movements of the actors.

Nevertheless the many illusionary devices made visible to the public a world of myth and magic and history and legend—a kind of supernature more dreamt about than experienced, giving intensity and color to the action, and locating it in an imaginary realm. A superreality, an allegorical verisimilitude was the stage designer's objective, as it was that of the geographical descriptions; by associating man and his actions with an exotic or splendid setting, his importance and uniqueness were magnified. There was no attempt to explain man in terms of environmental influences, though astrological influences were generally acknowledged.

It was characteristic of the period that it defined the word *landscape* in another manner: *landscape* indicated both the *background* of a picture, and a stage set—that element in a composition which gave it form and suggested location but which was not of the main body of the argument.

It was while this reverent and uncritical acceptance of the world prevailed that men expressed most eloquently their delight in God's creation; in painting, in writing, in the design of gardens and in the artificial world of the theater. The familiar landscape was thought to be no less worthy of study and admiration than the remote and new, and provincial culture flourished as vigorously as the metropolitan. It was in consequence a time when geographical descriptive writing enjoyed much the same sort of popularity as did the theater. A seventeenth-century French book on the art of conversation ridiculed the amateur geographer who, when he had bought a beaver hat, regaled his dinner companions with a discourse on Canada, the fur-trapping industry, discussed North and South America, naming their principal rivers and gold mines, adding details about their unusual flora and fauna. Atlases and albums of city panoramas were widely sold; fashionable ladies read books about Persia and Siam in order to shine in society. The same writer cautioned women against appearing *too* geography-minded. "I permit them to use such words as *climate, zone,* and *isthmus*," he wrote, "and a few others, but I do not want them to terrify me by mentioning *longitudes* and *latitudes*."

Toward the middle of the seventeenth century the metaphor of landscape as theater quite abruptly and quite radically began to change its significance. Theater ceased to mean exclusively *spectacle* and came to mean *drama*, the analysis and solution of a problem. Landscape painting acquired, at least in its choice of subjects, a formal,

almost abstract quality; the plan, the detailed map replaced the panorama of the countryside and city, as if color to charm the eye had been drained from the view of the world. Increasingly it was presented in the black and white of the printed word or the steel engraving.

It was in fact in the mid-seventeenth century that geographers appear to have abandoned their exclusive interest in description based on observation and personal experience and to have turned their attention to what we would now call the earth sciences. There were practical as well as philosophical reasons for the shift. The greatest demand for geographical expertise came from merchants and traders engaged in foreign commerce, eager for more precise knowledge of tides and weather and currents and the location of safe harbors. Both in France and England the crown demanded geographical investigation of strategic and political problems. The emphasis accordingly moved to research, to measurement and theory, and there was a corresponding decrease in provincial or historical writing, with its moral and religious ingredient. On the continent the influence of Descartes on geology and meteorology encouraged the rejection of the Classical heritage, as well as a skeptical approach to local sources of information. Vision itself demanded a new, scientific perspective: that of the microscope and telescope.

This turning inward, away from the world as a spectacle revealing the divine order, was also characteristic of the late seventeenth-century theater. Instead of seeking to establish man's central place by means of spatial illusion, the theater now resorted to intellectual means, formulating with increasing precision the doctrine of the three unities: unity of time, of place, and of action, and rejecting the magic aspects of the theater, at least in the presentation of serious drama. Tragedy demanded a small, all but empty stage with a highly formalized background— a room in a palace, a public space in the city. "As phi-

losophers have divided the universe . . . into three regions," Hobbes wrote, "celestial, aerial and terrestrial, so
the poets . . . have lodged themselves in the three regions
of mankind, court, city, country . . . From hence pro-
ceeded three sorts of poesy, heroic, schematic, and pastoral." In the heroic or tragic production interaction
between the stage and the surrounding imaginary world
was reduced to a minimum, as if the century were de-
claring that man was most clearly himself, was best identified, when the influences of the legendary environments
of history and supernature were eliminated. Drama was
interaction with other persons, a psychological confrontation." "The tragic palace," a historian of the seventeenth-
century theater has remarked, "the simple decorated an-
techamber with four doors . . . make all action and drama
converge on a single point. These correspond to the se-
verity of a plot or story line where fate has confined the
protagonists to one place and condemned them to struggle against each other until death—or flight—has liber-
ated them." "The bare stage epitomizes the new abstract
definition of space.

Thus with the development of a more intellectual, scientific geography, and a more intellectual, psychological
type of drama the metaphor of landscape as theater ceased
to be useful or appropriate. There remains, however, as
a kind of epilogue, the story of its final eclipse.

The popular, as distinguished from the serious or Classical, theater in the seventeenth century continued to
rejoice in the spectacular. An increasingly exaggerated
celebration of the mythical historical landscape, particularly in opera and ballet, eventually led to even more
grandiose productions, with the result that on the popular
level the staging, the scenery—the landscape in the theater sense of the word—threatened to overwhelm the actors and their not very significant dilemmas. The
fascination with illusion inevitably led to a fascination

with deception. Plays of little quality went to infinite
pains to achieve meticulous realism in staging: scenery,
props, and costumes reproduced in pedantic detail regional or historical settings—China, the New World, ancient Greece, scenes from the Bible. Accents and gestures
sought to reinforce the illusion, and actors, like figures
in a historical pageant, were reduced to little more than
props. A century earlier the scenic environment, whether
on the stage or in the landscape, had served to highlight
and intensify the identity of the protagonists: now, identity was seen as a matter of conformity to a given environment, a blending into it.

We can, in fact, indicate with some precision the moment when this reversal was complete. In 1799, Robert
Fulton, the American inventor, brought the first large
diorama to Paris. A grandiose, circular panorama of New
World scenery, accurate in every detail and without the
disturbing presence of a single actor, it was an immediate
success. Within a short time a theater was opened, devoted exclusively to dioramas, one of its rules being that
no more than two actors were ever to be allowed to appear
in front of the scenery. The theater was dedicated "to the
reproduction on a theatrical scale of those views which
are most worthy of exciting public curiosity from the
historical and picturesque point of view."

Significantly enough, one of the men who helped or-
ganize the theater was Daguerre, soon to make a name
for himself as a pioneer photographer.

This first theater without actors, devoted to the display
of landscapes without people, marks the appearance of a
totally new definition of landscape: natural scenery which
man should not contaminate by his presence. It also marks
the appearance of a new kind of drama—one which takes
place in a domestic interior and involves domestic and
psychological problems, hidden from the public world.
And with the final rejection of the Classical metaphor

of landscape as theater the search was on for a new and more vivid way of defining the landscape.

We are still searching. All that we have so far come up with is an analogue of one sort or another, borrowed from biology or ecology or communication theory. When it is a matter of controlling or manipulating the environment, analogues can be extremely helpful, yet if we are again to learn how to respond emotionally and esthetically and morally to the landscape, we must find a metaphor—or several metaphors—drawn from our human experience. The fact that we have so far failed to do so is no cause for despair. As history should teach us, and particularly the history of art, it is largely a matter of chronological perspective. It was only in the nineteenth century that men perceived the rightness of the theater metaphor as applied to the sixteenth- and seventeenth-century concept of landscape. It is only now that we are acquiring sufficient perspective on the nineteenth century to understand that landscape in terms of a metaphor of growth and decay and evolution. It is still too early to understand the new twentieth-century landscape. We can best rely on the insights of the geographer and the photographer and the philosopher. They are the most trustworthy custodians of the human tradition, for they seek to discover order within randomness, beauty within chaos, and the enduring aspirations of mankind behind blunders and failures.

Catalogue of the New Mexico
Photographic Survey

THOMAS F. BARROW

In the far northeast heights of Albuquerque there is a home worthy of the Universal Studios back lot. It is a deceptively ordinary suburban dwelling, but instead of the basic family unit it houses four Fairbanks-Morse pumps that help maintain water pressure for this section of the metropolitan system.

Water is an interesting subject in a high desert city. Although the primary water supply is from the ground, the storage is aboveground. This storage is in large, adobe-colored tanks that ring the city, often in the most unlikely locations, surrounded by the effluvia typical of unbridled and unzoned sunbelt growth. We might see these tanks and their hidden conduits as the underlying matrix of Albuquerque's growth structure. They and their life-supporting contents cannot be blamed for the appearance of their general environs. There are larger issues responsible for that, and not only in Albuquerque.

Thomas F. Barrow's photographic work is widely exhibited and published. Former student of Aaron Siskind, he teaches at the University of New Mexico and has received National Endowment fellowships for his work. He writes and lectures on contemporary work as well as on the history of photography. He coedited *Reading into Photography, Selected Writings, 1959–81.* His work is represented in numerous private and public collections including the San Francisco Museum of Modern Art, the International Museum of Photography at the George Eastman House, The Museum of Modern Art, the University of New Mexico Art Museum, the Museum of New Mexico, the Center for Creative Photography, and the Sheldon Memorial Art Gallery.

PROCESS: Sepia-toned gelatin silver photographs with
Polaroid photographs attached

From the Series "Water as Matrix," Albuquerque:

1. College well and reservoir, 1983
13⁵/₁₆ × 19⁵/₁₆   7 Polaroids: 3¹/₈ × 3¹/₁₆
33.8 × 49.1   7.9 × 7.7

2. *Conrad I. Gonzales Central Control, looking east, 1983*
13⁷/₁₆ × 19³/₈   4 Polaroids: 3¹/₈ × 3¹/₁₆
34.1 × 49.2   7.9 × 7.7

*Image used as plate in text.

89

3. *Thomas Well #1 Reservoir, 1983*
   13¹/₄ × 19⁵/₁₆   4 Polaroids: 3¹/₈ × 3¹/₁₆
   33.6 × 49.1   7.9 × 7.7

5. *Leyendecker Pump Station and Reservoir, looking north, 1983*
   13³/₁₆ × 19⁵/₁₆   4 Polaroids: 3¹/₈ × 3¹/₁₆
   33.5 × 49.1   7.9 × 7.7

4. *Don Reservoir, 1983*
   13¹/₂ × 19⁵/₁₆   4 Polaroids: 3¹/₈ × 3¹/₁₆
   33.6 × 49.1   7.9 × 7.7

6. *Yale Pump Station and Reservoir, 1983*
   13³/₈ × 19⁵/₁₆   4 Polaroids: 3¹/₈ × 3¹/₁₆
   34 × 49.1   7.9 × 7.7

*7. Franciscan Reservoir, 1983
13³/₈ × 19⁵/₁₆   4 Polaroids: 3¹/₈ × 3¹/₁₆
34 × 49.1   7.9 × 7.7

9. San Jose Reservoir and Pump Station, South Broadway, 1983
13⁵/₁₆ × 19⁵/₁₆   4 Polaroids: 3¹/₈ × 3¹/₁₆
33.8 × 49.1   10.8 × 8.9

8. Miles Reservoir, 1983
13³/₁₆ × 19⁵/₁₆   4 Polaroids: 3¹/₈ × 3¹/₁₆
33.5 × 49.1   10.8 × 8.9

10. Santa Barbara Well, looking east, 1983
13⁷/₁₆ × 19⁵/₁₆   4 Polaroids: 3¹/₈ × 3¹/₁₆
34.1 × 49.1   10.8 × 8.9

MIGUEL GANDERT

Albuquerque's South Valley is a world of dualities. It is the place where the rural world of the Rio Grande Valley and the urban expansions of Albuquerque meet. Even though the downtown area is rapidly changing and growing, the surrounding communities are among the oldest and most traditional in Albuquerque.

In these images I have tried to create honest portraits. I hope this examination of people, their gestures, and the way they relate to their environment will reveal a unique part of the city.

Miguel Gandert is a freelance photographer, news production manager and videographer for KOAT-TV in Albuquerque. His work is exhibited internationally and included in collections of the Museum of New Mexico, the Art Museum and Special Collections Library of the University of New Mexico.

*1. *Bathers, First Plaza, Albuquerque, 1983*
12½ × 18¾
31.7 × 47.6

*2. *Anthony, Georgia, Joseph, and Ruby Hernandez, South Williams Street SE, Albuquerque, 1983*
12½ × 18¾
31.7 × 47.6

PROCESS: Selenium-toned chloro-bromide photographs

3. *Brothers, Coal Ave. SE, Albuquerque, 1983*
12¹/₂ × 18⁵/₈
31.7 × 47.3

4. *Priscilla, Paulette, and Martha Stevens, South Broadway,*
Albuquerque, 1983
12¹/₂ × 18³/₄
31.7 × 47.6

5. *Reuben Garcia, San José, Albuquerque, 1983*
12¹/₂ × 18⁵/₈
31.7 × 47.3

6. *Steven and Orlando Molina, Rio Bravo Blvd., Albuquerque,*
1983
12¹/₂ × 18³/₄
31.7 × 47.6

7. *Henry Alderete and Arno Garcia, San José, Albuquerque, 1983*
12¹/₂ × 18³/₄
31.7 × 47.6

9. *Al Hurricane and Charlie Burke, Northwestern Corral, Albuquerque, 1983*
12¹/₂ × 18³/₄
31.7 × 47.6

8. *Richard Mares and Seferino Lucero, Rio Bravo Blvd., Albuquerque, 1983*
12¹/₂ × 18⁵/₈
31.7 × 47.3

*10. *Melissa Armijo, Eloy Montoya, and Richard "El Wino" Madrid, Albuquerque, 1983*
12⁵/₈ × 18⁷/₈
32 × 47.9

11. *Woman Welder, Coal Blvd. and Interstate 25, Albuquerque, 1983*
12^7/$_{16}$ × 18^5/$_8$
31.6 × 47.3

13. *Adam and Eden King, Lomas Blvd. NW, Albuquerque, 1983*
18^3/$_4$ × 12^9/$_{16}$
47.6 × 31.8

12. *Melissa Armijo, San José, Albuquerque, 1983*
18^3/$_4$ × 12^9/$_{16}$
47.6 × 31.8

14. *Renee Carmona and Melissa Armijo, South Broadway, Albuquerque, 1983*
12^1/$_2$ × 18^1/$_2$
31.7 × 47

15. *Leroy Romero, San José, Albuquerque, 1983*
    12⁵/₈ × 18³/₄
    32 × 47.6

16. *Greg Mora, San José, Albuquerque, 1983*
    12¹/₄ × 18³/₄
    31.1 × 47.6

ALEX HARRIS

The mountain villages of the Sangre de Cristo range are the quintessential communities of the Hispanic Southwest. These are the places where traditional culture survives, if not intact, then at least in many of its important manifestations. What remains is not something preserved for the sake of tourism, and even those elements that have merged with the dominant culture are deeply tied to their traditional roots.

Over the last two years, I have photographed in dozens of these Hispanic villages that surround my home in northern New Mexico. Bounded on the north and east by the Picuris range and the Mora Valley, and on the south and west by Glorieta Mesa and the Rio Grande, this area for me has come to resemble—both literally and metaphorically—an island. While the currents of mainstream America have washed over everything else around it, this rugged and isolated highland continues to rise quite proudly and sometimes defiantly above the tides.

As a photographer, I hope that the people, noticeably absent in these pictures, will be reflected in their distinctive esthetic, in the bold and eloquent decorations of their homes and villages, and that some of my affection for them and for this place will be evident as well.

Alexander Harris studied psychology at Yale University and is director of the Center for Documentary Photography at Duke University. He has received fellowships from the Rockefeller and John Simon Guggenheim Memorial foundations and has edited numerous documentary publications. His work is represented in collections of The Museum of Modern Art, the High Museum of Art, the Addison Gallery of American Art, and the Museum of New Mexico.

1. *Bialquín Pacheco's house, Vallecito, August 1981*
   15 × 19 1/4
   38.1 × 48.9

2. *Rio Lucio, June 1981*
   15 1/4 × 19 1/4
   38.8 × 48.9

PROCESS: Ektacolor 78RC photographs

3. *Las Trampas, March 1982*
   40 × 50
   101.6 × 127

5. *Chamisal, December 1981*
   15¹/₂ × 19¹/₈
   38.5 × 48.6

*4. *Truchas, June 1982*
   14¹³/₁₆ × 18³/₄
   37.6 × 47.5

*6. *Rio Lucio, June 1982*
   15³/₈ × 19
   39.1 × 48.3

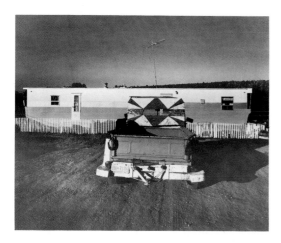

7. *Peñasco, June 1981*
   15³/₈ × 19
   39.1 × 48.3

9. *El Valle, June 1981*
   15³/₈ × 19
   39.1 × 48.3

8. *Sahd's Store, Peñasco, June 1981*
   19 × 15
   48.2 × 38.1

10. *Wagon Wheel Bar, Llano Largo, March 1982*
    15¹/₈ × 19³/₈
    38.9 × 49.2

11. *My front porch, El Valle, March 1982*
   15¹/₄ × 19³/₈
   38.8 × 49.2

13. *Las Vegas, June 1982*
   19 × 15³/₈
   39.1 × 48.3

12. *Onesimo Pacheco's house, Vallecito, July 1981*
   14¹⁵/₁₆ × 18¹⁵/₁₆
   38 × 48.1

14. *Rodarte, June 1981*
   15³/₈ × 19
   39.1 × 48.3

15. *Las Vegas, June 1982*
    15³/₈ × 19
    39.1 × 48.3

PAUL LOGSDON

From the air, New Mexico's arid landscape conceals little. In more verdant climates, lush growth quickly reclaims disturbed land, and in many cases, even massive construction projects, as in Meso-America or Southeast Asia.

History is laid bare here. From ancient ruins to urban sprawl, the efforts of humans to accommodate to this place are revealed in sharp relief. Cultural values and influences are quite evident, with rapid growth producing drastic changes in long-established patterns. This unique perspective of the human landscape in New Mexico helps create an unparalleled picture and document of our times.

Paul Logsdon, formerly a test pilot and photo-reconnaissance pilot, exhibits regionally and has produced work for the British Broadcasting Company, Time-Life Books, the American Federation of Arts, the Archeological Conservancy, and the School of American Research. His work is included in the collections of the Museum of New Mexico and Sunwest Bank of Santa Fe.

PROCESS: Cibachrome II color photographs

*1. *Chetro Ketl, Chaco Canyon, 1982*
15 × 19
38.1 × 48.3

2. *Pueblo Colorado, Galisteo Basin, 1982*
15 × 19
38.1 × 48.3

102

3. *Gran Quivira, Salinas National Monument, 1982*
15 × 19
38.1 × 48.3

4. *Kwastiyukwa, Pueblo ruins in Jemez Mountains, 1982*
19 × 15
48.3 × 38.1

Indian Community

5. *Football practice at Laguna Pueblo, 1982*
40 × 50
101.6 × 127

6. *Navajo settlement, San Juan Basin Checkerboard Area, 1982*
15 × 19
38.1 × 48.3

*7. *Zia Pueblo, 1982*
   19⁷/₁₆ × 15¹/₄
   49.4 × 38.8

8. *Acoma Pueblo with Enchanted Mesa, 1982*
   18¹⁵/₁₆ × 15
   48.1 × 38.1

9. *Santo Domingo Pueblo, 1982*
   15 × 19
   38.1 × 48.3

Water

10. *Peñasco Spring, Sierra Nacimiento, 1982*
   7¹/₁₆ × 8¹⁵/₁₆
   17.9 × 22.7

11. *Elephant Butte Reservoir, 1982*
8¹⁵/₁₆ × 7¹/₁₆
22.7 × 17.9

13. *Cañada Estacada, Santa Fe County, 1982*
8¹⁵/₁₆ × 7¹/₁₆
22.7 × 17.9

12. *Salinas Lakes, Torrance County, 1982*
7¹/₁₆ × 8¹⁵/₁₆
17.9 × 22.7

14. *Chino Mine, Santa Rita, New Mexico, 1982*
7¹/₁₆ × 8¹⁵/₁₆
17.9 × 22.7

Farm Land

15. *Anasazi farms, Jemez Mountains, 1982*
   $7^1/_{16} \times 9$
   17.9×22.8

16. *Triangle harvest, plains of San Augustin, 1982*
   $7^1/_8 \times 9$
   18.1×22.8

17. *Forked Lightning Ranch, Pecos, 1982*
   $7^1/_{16} \times 9$
   17.9×22.8

18. *Abandoned homestead, Stanley, 1982*
   $7^1/_{16} \times 9$
   17.9×22.8

106

Enclaves

19. *Plaza del Cerro, Chimayo, 1982*
    15 × 19
    38.1 × 48.3

20. *Dar-al-Islam Mosque and school, Abiquiu, 1982*
    14⁷/₈ × 19
    37.8 × 48.3

21. *Santa Fe custom adobe, 1982*
    15 × 19
    38.1 × 48.3

City

22. *Automobile row, Albuquerque, Lomas and University, 1982*
    7¹/₁₆ × 9
    17.9 × 22.8.

23. *State Fair midway, Albuquerque, 1982*
    9 × 7¹/₁₆
    22.8 × 17.9

24. *Country Club Gardens, Santa Fe, 1982*
    7¹/₁₆ × 9
    17.9 × 22.8

JOAN MYERS

In 1822 William Becknell led the first freight wagons from Franklin, Missouri, through southern Kansas, down across northeastern New Mexico to Santa Fe, thus establishing the viability of a trade route soon known as the Santa Fe Trail. Thousands of traders and immigrants along with United States Army troops traveled the trail until it was superseded by the railroad in 1880.

The Santa Fe Trail was never a tangible object, a clearly delineated marked road in the sense of a modern highway. Rather it was composed of ruts—sometimes a single set, often several more depending on the prevailing weather or the needs and whims of a particular caravan. For those who carved the deep ruts across the prairie and marveled at the primitive towns of New Mexico, the Santa Fe Trail was primarily a means to an end, a hope for the future, a dream of opportunity.

It was my challenge to photograph a feeling, an idea, a dream from the past using the landmarks of the trail and the tangible imagery of the present.

Joan Myers studied renaissance and baroque music at Stanford University before working in photography. Her photographic work is widely exhibited and represented in private and public collections, including the Bibliothèque Nationale, the Center for Creative Photography, the University of New Mexico Art Museum, the Museum of New Mexico, the Sheldon Memorial Art Gallery, and the Amon Carter Museum of Western Art.

*1. *San Miguel, New Mexico, 1982*
13 × 10⁵/₁₆
33 × 26.3

*2. *Raton Pass, New Mexico, 1982*
10³/₁₆ × 12¹⁵/₁₆
25.9 × 32.8

PROCESS: Platinum-palladium photographs with hand coloring

3. *Lower Spring, Kansas, 1982*
   13⁷/₁₆ × 10³/₁₆
   34.1 × 25.9

*5. *Round Mound, New Mexico, 1982*
   9¹⁵/₁₆ × 12⁷/₈
   25.2 × 32.7

4. *Inscription Rock, Oklahoma, 1982*
   10¹/₈ × 13
   25.7 × 33

6. *Bent's New Fort, Colorado, 1982*
   10¹/₄ × 13¹/₄
   26.7 × 33.6

7. *Bent's Old Fort, Colorado, 1982*
   9⁷/₈ × 12¹/₄
   24.7 × 31.1

9. *Tecolote, New Mexico, 1982*
   10¹/₈ × 13
   25.7 × 30.3

8. *Fort Union, New Mexico, 1982*
   12⁹/₁₆ × 9⁷/₈
   31.9 × 25.1

10. *San José, New Mexico, 1982*
    9⁷/₈ × 13
    25.1 × 33

111

11. *Pecos, New Mexico, 1982*
    10¹/₄ × 12³/₈
    26 × 31.4

12. *Cañoncito, New Mexico, 1982*
    10⁷/₁₆ × 12³/₄
    26.5 × 32.3

13. *Santa Fe from Fort Marcy (triptych), 1982*
    5⁷/₈ × 22³/₄
    14.9 × 57.7

ANNE NOGGLE

I am intrigued by the otherness of people, in the sense
that everything outside my skin is foreign.
Photographing is my means of making them visible,
accessible, and available—hoping by this peculiar,
enforced isolation to reveal something otherwise
unknowable. The knowable factor is that the people in
these photographs are all New Mexicans. This might
have been a unifying tie, but instead each is individual,
withholding, outreaching, tense, open, vibrant, or
hidden as is their wont. They have given this
photographer as much challenge as people anywhere,
and also a pleasurable sigh of relief that some form of
cloning has not taken place, that human uniqueness is
alive and well and living in New Mexico.

*1. *Rosa Wiley, seamstress, 1982*
    16 × 11¹¹/₁₆
    40.6 × 29.7

Anne Noggle exhibits and lectures internationally on her
work. She has received fellowships from the John Simon
Guggenheim Memorial Foundation and the National
Endowment for the Arts. Her portraits have been published
in a monograph, *Silver Lining,* and are represented in the
collections of the San Francisco Museum of Modern Art, the
International Museum of Photography at the George
Eastman House, the University of New Mexico Art Museum,
the Museum of New Mexico, and the Houston Museum of
Fine Arts.

2. *Henry Bumkens, detective, 1981*
   16¹/₈ × 11⁷/₈
   41 × 30.1

PROCESS: Gelatin silver photographs

*3. *J. B. Jackson, cultural geographer, 1983*
16 × 11⁵/₁₆
40.6 × 28.7

5. *Helen Hobart, 1982*
12 × 16¹/₈
30.5 × 41

4. *Don Kuzio, 1983*
16¹/₁₆ × 10⁷/₈
40.7 × 27.6

6. *Mary, 1981*
15⁵/₁₆ × 10³/₈
38.9 × 26.4

7. *Donna Humble, copywriter, 1983*
   11¹/₄ × 16¹/₈
   28.5 × 41

9. *Edith Buchanan, professor emeritus, 1981*
   15⁹/₁₆ × 11⁷/₈
   40.3 × 30.3

8. *Edith "Tiny" Keene, 1981*
   15⁷/₈ × 11¹⁵/₁₆
   40.3 × 30.3

10. *Winnie Beasley, flyer, 1983*
    11¹/₈ × 16¹/₈
    28.2 × 41

11. *Charles Mattox, sculptor, and his wife, Dorothy, 1982*
    12 × 16¹/₁₆
    30.5 × 40.8

13. *Margaret Walch, writer, 1982*
    16⁵/₁₆ × 12¹/₄
    43 × 31.1

12. *Profile of Yolanda, 1982*
    15³/₄ × 12¹/₂
    40 × 31.7

14. *Margaret Stratton, graduate student, 1982*
    16⁷/₁₆ × 11³/₈
    41.7 × 28.9

116

15. *K. Y. Haaland, neuropsychologist, 1982*
    $11^{15}/_{16} \times 15^{15}/_{16}$
    30.3×40.5

MARY PECK

"... a treeless, desolate waste of uninhabited solitude, which always has been, and must continue, uninhabited forever ..."

—"The Report of Capt. R. B. Marcy's Route from Fort Smith to Santa Fe," 1850

Ever since travelers began recording comments on eastern New Mexico and west Texas, most reactions have been unfavorable. This land has none of the things to offer that most people associate with a beautiful or grand landscape. There is no place for the eye to rest, no seeming point of interest. One leaves this area with the feeling that there is nothing there to own. One is left in this land with nothing to experience but the land itself and the glorious unending horizon.

Mary Peck assisted and studied with photographers Laura Gilpin and Paul Caponigro. Her work is exhibited nationally and is included in collections of the Houston Museum of Fine Arts, the Museum of New Mexico, Notre Dame University Art Gallery, and the Amon Carter Museum of Western Art.

1. *C. S. Cattle Company, near Miami, New Mexico, 1982*
   8 × 10
   20.3 × 25.4

*2. *Lake bed, Palo Blanco, New Mexico, 1983*
   6 × 15
   15.2 × 38.1

PROCESS: Toned gelatin silver photographs

3. *Roy, New Mexico, 1981*
   8 × 10
   20.3 × 25.4

5. *House Public School, House, New Mexico, 1983*
   8 × 10
   20.3 × 25.4

*4. *Near Maes, New Mexico, 1983*
   6 × 15
   15.2 × 38.1

6. *Yeso, New Mexico, 1982*
   8 × 10
   20.3 × 25.4

7. *Near Dalhart, Texas, 1981*
   8 × 10
   20.3 × 25.4

9. *South Second Street, Tucumcari, New Mexico, 1983*
   8 × 10
   20.3 × 25.4

8. *Highway 39, Mosquero, New Mexico, 1983*
   8 × 10
   20.3 × 25.4

10. *Near Clayton, New Mexico, 1982*
    8 × 10
    20.3 × 25.4

11. *Pecos Valley Cotton Oil Inc., Loving, New Mexico, 1983*
    6 × 15
    15.2 × 38.1

14. *Chaves County Cattle Company, near Roswell, New Mexico,*
    1983
    6 × 15
    15.2 × 38.1

12. *Pecan orchard, Roswell, New Mexico, 1983*
    6 × 15
    15.2 × 38.1

15. *Junction, County Road No. 741 and No. 742, near Loving,*
    New Mexico, 1983
    6 × 15
    15.2 × 38.1

13. *Potash refinery, near Carlsbad, New Mexico, 1983*
    6 × 15
    15.2 × 38.1

16. *Yates Petroleum Company, exploratory well, west of*
    Lovington, New Mexico, 1983
    6 × 15
    15.2 × 38.1

121

17. *Alex Griego, San Miguel County Commissioner, near Maes,*
New Mexico, 1983
6 × 15
15.2 × 38.1

20. *Black River Village, New Mexico, 1983*
6 × 15
15.2 × 38.1

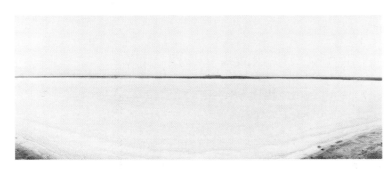

*18. *Salt beds, near Loving, New Mexico, 1983*
6 × 15
15.2 × 38.1

19. *Potash refinery, near Carlsbad, New Mexico, 1983*
6 × 15
15.2 × 38.1

122

BERNARD PLOSSU

It's a warm day in Columbus. No people to photograph in the streets. Too hot! How much I love being there, right by Mexico, in that immense Southwest that I saw as a child on cinemascope screens on rainy afternoons of Parisian Sundays. Now, it is the real thing! Especially here, in southern New Mexico, where things haven't changed much, except the one big highway that goes from Texas to California. But the people who drive on it just stop overnight, in Deming or Lordsburg, and go by without realizing how great it actually is. If only they knew!

I have been attracted to this empty area since the mid-sixties, and I keep going back.

Noncurious people could say there is nothing there, just dust, wind, tumbleweeds. But there is so much—the feeling of freedom, the voice of silence, and also a haunting presence of history, of the Apache raids, of Pancho Villa. The border has a fascinating past, and there too, the three cultures are present.

This southern part of our state is such a real New Mexico. Just as it was last century, it is still now!

Bernard Plossu lectures frequently on his work, which is exhibited and published internationally. He has had two monographs published: *Egypte* and *New Mexico Revisited.* His work is represented in collections of the Bibliothèque Nationale, Stedelijk Museum, the International Museum of Photography at the George Eastman House, the Museum of New Mexico, the Center for Creative Photography, the Sheldon Memorial Art Gallery, and the Amon Carter Museum of Western Art.

PROCESS: Gelatin silver photographs (1–11); Fresson color prints (12–17)

*1. *Sunset and dust, rodeo south of Animas (southern New Mexico), 1981*
8 × 11¹⁵/₁₆
20.3 × 30.3

*2. *Way down, south of Animas, close to Mexico (Route 338), 1981*
8 × 11¹⁵/₁₆
20.3 × 30.3

3. *A house in Hachita, 1981*
    12 × 8
    30.5 × 20.3

4. *Landscape south of Las Cruces, 1981*
    7⁷/₈ × 11³/₄
    20.1 × 30.1

5. *Silence, all the way south, far, 1981*
    11³/₄ × 7⁷/₈
    30.1 × 20

6. *Animas store, 1981*
    11¹³/₁₆ × 8
    30.3 × 20.3

7. *Around Deming, 1981*
   8 × 11⁷/₈
   20.3 × 30.3

9. *Night race in Alamogordo, 1981*
   8 × 11¹⁵/₁₆
   20.3 × 30.3

8. *Lasso—Rodeo south of Animas, 1981*
   8 × 11¹⁵/₁₆
   20.3 × 30.3

10. *Rodeo south of Animas, 1981*
    8 × 11¹⁵/₁₆
    20.3 × 30.3

11. *The street in Hachita, 1981*
    8 × 11¹⁵/₁₆
    20.3 × 30.3

13. *Deming, 1981*
    7³/₈ × 10¹³/₁₆
    18.7 × 27.5

12. *Deming, 1981*
    7³/₈ × 10¹³/₁₆
    18.7 × 27.5

14. *Deming, 1981*
    7³/₈ × 10¹³/₁₆
    18.7 × 27.5

15. *Deming, 1981*
    7³/₈ × 10¹³/₁₆
    18.7 × 27.5

17. *Lordsburg, 1981*
    7³/₈ × 10¹³/₁₆
    18.7 × 27.5

16. *Deming, 1981*
    7³/₈ × 10¹³/₁₆
    18.7 × 27.5

EDWARD RANNEY

At a time when much contemporary art and technology seem only tenuously related to our most pressing cultural and spiritual concerns, it is important to remember, as one historian has remarked, that "ruins are never the records of total strangers." As archaeological sites are alternately destroyed, over-visited, or neglected, our photographs of them must now often stand for the sites themselves as well as intuit how light, space, and structure gave shape in the primal mind to cultural and calendrical form.

Equally important is a visual archaeology of our own time, one conceived with what might be called a sense of archaeology in reverse. The earth sculpture Charles Ross is constructing in eastern New Mexico is conceived as a naked-eye observatory focusing on Polaris and the relationship of human form to cosmic time and space. To photograph the growth of this site is to participate in the creation of a complex cultural and perceptual space. As such it is a metaphor, as J. B. Jackson affirms in *The Necessity for Ruins*, for a context that physically and spiritually reengages us, after a period of disruption and discontinuity, in order to "reproduce the cosmic scheme and correct history."

Edward Ranney's photographic work is widely published and exhibited. He has received fellowships from the John Simon Guggenheim Memorial Foundation, Fulbright, and the National Endowment for the Arts. His work is included in the collections of the Victoria and Albert Museum, the Museum of Modern Art, the Museum of New Mexico, the Art Institute of Chicago, and the Amon Carter Museum of Western Art. Among his books are *Stonework of the Maya* and *Monuments of the Incas.*

1. *Star Axis, looking east, 1982*
   6¹/₂ × 9¹/₂
   14.6 × 21.6

2. *Star Axis, looking north, 1/6/83*
   10⁵/₈ × 15
   29.5 × 38.1

PROCESS: Selenium-toned gelatin silver photographs

128

3. *Star Axis, looking north, 1/7/83*
6½ × 9½
14.6 × 21.6

*5. *Star Axis, looking south, 1/7/83*
10½ × 15
26.7 × 38.1

4. *Star Axis, looking north, 1/7/83*
6½ × 9½
14.6 × 21.6

6. *Star Axis, looking south, 8/26/83*
10½ × 15
26.7 × 38.1

*7. *Cochiti Lake, 1983*
10³/₄ × 15¹/₄
27.3 × 38.7

*9. *Hungo Pavi to Fajada Butte, Chaco Canyon, 1982*
10¹/₂ × 15
26.7 × 38.1

8. *Cochiti Dam, 1983*
11 × 16¹/₂
28 × 41.9

10. *Dar-al-Islam, Abiquiu, 1982*
6¹/₂ × 9¹/₂
14.6 × 21.6

11. *Pueblo Bonito, Chaco Canyon, 1982*
    6¹/₂ × 9¹/₂
    14.6 × 21.6

12. *Hungo Pavi, Chaco Canyon, 1982*
    6¹/₂ × 9¹/₂
    14.6 × 21.6

13. *Chino Mine, Santa Rita, 1983*
    11¹/₄ × 16¹/₄
    28.6 × 41.3

14. *Very Large Array, near Mogollon, 1982*
    10³/₄ × 15¹/₂
    27.3 × 39.4

131

MERIDEL RUBENSTEIN

The Lord blesseth the habitation of the just.

—Prov. iii, 33

I chose for the Survey to photograph three sites that
exemplify different dwelling modes in New Mexico—
the Native American pueblo (Paguate at Laguna
Pueblo), the rural Hispanic village (Wagon Mound), and
the ranch cluster (Progresso, near Willard). These
places are in varying stages of old age and disuse.

I wanted to examine the basic dwellings and village
structures and the changes over time of these habitats.
The exposures were made in sequences because the
lives of these remarkable places, from my limited
vantage point, seemed to exist at once in the past,
present, and future—each with its own fiction as well
as its own reality.

Meridel Rubenstein's photographic work is widely
exhibited and published. Former student of Minor White, she
has received fellowships from the John Simon Guggenheim
Memorial Foundation and the National Endowment for the
Arts as well as the Ferguson Grant from the Friends of
Photography. She teaches and lectures on photography across
the country, and her work is represented in collections of the
San Francisco Museum of Modern Art, the Center for
Creative Photography, the University of New Mexico Art
Museum, the Museum of New Mexico, the Minneapolis
Institute of Arts, and the Denver Art Museum.

*1. *The sheep camp at Mesita in Laguna Pueblo, 1982–83*
   15¹/₄ × 15³/₈
   38.7 × 39.1

2. *Dissolving Mesa, Mesita Village at Laguna Pueblo, 1982–83*
   22 × 30
   55.9 × 76.2

PROCESS: Ektacolor 74RC photographs mounted on
          Fabriano hot-press watercolor paper

132

3. *Anaconda Miles at Paguate in Laguna Pueblo with Poem by Harold Littlebird, 1982–83*
   18 × 14¹/₂
   45.7 × 36.8

4. *A senior citizen made these shelters at Paguate in Laguna Pueblo, 1982–83*
   12³/₄ × 18
   32.4 × 45.7

*5. *The Swallow's House, Progresso, 1982–83*
   15³/₄ × 24⁵/₁₆
   40 × 64.3

6. *Past and present owners of "The Macario Torres Place," Progresso, 1982–83*
   22 × 30
   55.9 × 76.2

7. *Fred and Maria Luna, 1982–83*
   22 × 30
   55.9 × 76.2

8. *The Single Woman's House, Progresso, 1982–83*
   22 × 30
   55.9 × 76.2

9. *Delpha Graham and son, "All my dreams are of this place,"*
   Progresso, 1982–83
   15 × 16
   38.1 × 40.6

10. *The Patron Saint of Wagon Mound in Santa Clara, 1982–83*
    22 × 30
    55.9 × 76.2

11. *Siting the Wagon Mound, 1982–83*
    22 × 30
    55.9 × 76.2

12. *Wagon Mound, New Mexico, 1982–83*
    22 × 30
    55.9 × 76.2

RICHARD WICKSTROM

This project is an exploration of transitional spaces in southern New Mexico cities, particularly in new suburban areas where alterations of the land exist almost exclusively as a result of economic biases. Traditionally, light, color, and regional subjects of the Southwest have been the pictorial elements used by artists to reveal romantic notions about New Mexico. Today, the Southwest is faced with increasing socioeconomic pressures and change, which have transformed its living character. In my work, these elements reveal a new relationship where the temporality of modern building and the beauty of New Mexico's light-revealing color expresses, in part, the ambiguities of our time.

Richard Wickstrom is president and senior printer of Lightworks of Santa Fe, Inc. Formerly a contemporary art curator, he lectures and exhibits his work regionally. His work is included in collections of the University of Iowa, the Museum of New Mexico and the U.S. Information Agency.

*1. *El Pueblo, West Mesa Subdivision, Las Cruces, 1982*
14^{15}/$_{16}$ × 18^{15}/$_{16}$
38 × 48.1

*2. *East Mesa Construction, Las Cruces, 1982*
14^{15}/$_{16}$ × 19
38 × 48.2

PROCESS: Ektacolor 74RC and 78RC photographs

3. *Entry Way, West Mesa Subdivision, Las Cruces, 1982*
14³/₄ × 19¹/₈
37.5 × 48.6

5. *Terrace Hill Mobile Home Park, East Mesa,*
Las Cruces, 1982
14¹⁵/₁₆ × 19
38 × 48.2

4. *Courtyard, West Mesa Subdivision, Las Cruces, 1982*
14¹⁵/₁₆ × 18¹⁵/₁₆
38 × 48.1

6. *Home, West Mesa Subdivision, Las Cruces, 1982*
15 × 19¹/₈
38.1 × 48.5

7. *Roswell Construction Site, Southwest Side, 1982*
15³/₁₆ × 18¹/₂
38.5 × 47

8. *Golf Course and House, West Mesa, Las Cruces, 1982*
15 × 18¹¹/₁₆
38 × 47.5

9. *Intersection of Mt. View and Mt. Shadow Drive, East Mesa, Las Cruces, 1981*
15 × 19¹/₈
38.1 × 48.6

10. *Power Lines, East Mesa, Las Cruces, 1981*
15 × 15³/₄
38.1 × 40.1

11. *Factory Under Construction, Las Cruces, 1981*
    12³/₈ × 19¹/₈
    31.4 × 48.6

13. *Neo-Adobe Home Under Construction, West Mesa
    Subdivision, Las Cruces, 1982*
    15¹/₁₆ × 19¹/₈
    38.2 × 48.6

12. *Cul-de-sac, East Mesa, Las Cruces, 1981*
    12³/₈ × 19
    31.4 × 48.2

RICHARD WILDER

My interest in photographing Santa Fe began several years ago, upon seeing a local exhibit that combined historical and contemporary photographs of the city. These photographs made clear the ongoing process of change. At this point in Santa Fe's history, change is of urgent interest, for the pace of change seems to have greatly accelerated in the last few years. It seemed to me possible to document in a very short time changes as great as those over the much longer time span of the earlier exhibit. The more I worked, however, the more aware I became of the possibility of suggesting some of the political, social, and cultural forces that are both cause and effect in this endless process of change. The attempt to deal with these issues as well as visual ones was both the struggle and reward that kept this project exciting and alive for me.

Richard Wilder is a student of Paul Caponigro. He exhibits nationally and is represented in collections of the Santa Barbara Museum of Art, the University of Notre Dame Art Gallery, and the Museum of New Mexico.

PROCESS: Gold-toned gelatin silver photographs

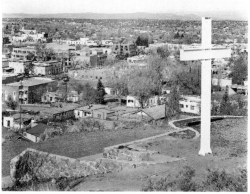

1. *Downtown, Santa Fe, 1983*
   Looking southwest, Hillside Park
   Looking southwest, Paseo de Peralta
   Looking southwest, Cross of the Martyrs
   (3 Photographs)
   7¹/₂ × 9¹/₂
   19.1 × 24.2

*2. *125 West Water Street, February 1982*
   125 West Water Street, August 1983
   (2 Photographs)
   7¹/₂ × 9¹/₂
   19.1 × 24.2

3. *207 West San Francisco Street, February 1982*
   207 West San Francisco Street, August 1983
   (2 Photographs)
   7¹/₂ × 9¹/₂
   19.1 × 24.2

5. *221 Galisteo Street, October 1982*
   221 Galisteo Street, August 1983
   (2 Photographs)
   7½ × 9½
   19.1 × 24.2

6. *New development, looking east on*
   Lincoln Avenue, January 1982
   New development, looking east on
   Lincoln Avenue, November 1982
   (2 Photographs)
   7½ × 9½
   19.1 × 24.2

4. *Landscapes, Santa Fe, 1983*
   Looking southeast of Old Taos Highway, north side, Santa Fe
   Looking north of hill above Camino Santander, east side, Santa Fe
   Looking north along Yucca Street, south side, Santa Fe
   Looking south across Agua Fria Street, west side, Santa Fe
   (4 Photographs)
   $7^1/_2 \times 9^1/_2$
   19.1 × 24.2

7. *751 Acequia Madre Street, Nos. 1–6,*
   January 1982
   751 Acequia Madre Street, Nos. 1–6,
   November 1982
   (2 Photographs)
   $7^1/_2 \times 9^1/_2$
   19.1 × 24.2

8. *New development, looking west on*
   Washington Avenue, October 1982
   New development, looking west on
   Washington Avenue, April 1983
   (2 Photographs)
   $7^1/_2 \times 9^1/_2$
   19.1 × 24.2

9. *95 West Marcy Avenue (Josie's Casa de Comida), 1983*
110 West San Francisco (Santa Fe Cookie Company), 1983
(2 Photographs)
7¹/₂ × 9¹/₂
19.1 × 24.2

10. *1836 Cerrillos Road (Ace Auto Supply), 1983*
135 West Palace Avenue (Cecil Sherwood's Chevron Station), 1983
(2 Photographs)
7¹/₂ × 9¹/₂
19.1 × 24.2

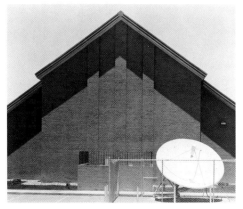

11. *401 Old Santa Fe Trail (rear of San Miguel Mission), 1982*
410 Rodeo Road (rear of Church of Jesus Christ of Latter Day Saints Stake Center), 1983
(2 Photographs)
7¹/₂ × 9¹/₂
19.1 × 24.2

12. *408 Rosario Lane (residence), 1981*
    548 Agua Fria Street (restaurant),
    1981
    (2 Photographs)
    7¹/₂ × 9¹/₂
    19.1 × 24.2

13. *Amelia Beard Hollenback House,*
    north of Sunmount (John Gaw Meem,
    architect), 1983
    West view from portal
    Portal
    (2 Photographs)
    7¹/₂ × 9¹/₂
    19.1 × 24.2

*14. *Archaeological dig, Washington Avenue*
    Development, 1982
    Adobe construction, near Santa Fe, 1983
    (2 Photographs)
    7¹/₂ × 9¹/₂
    19.1 × 24.2

Acknowledgments

To request that a writer or photographer produce discerning works about a common subject—particularly in light of its unique and remarkable traditions—is an adventurous proposition. I am indebted to J. B. Jackson and to these photographers who regard New Mexico with the deepest commitments, for their findings provide an uncommonly perceptive understanding of this place. This book of essays and works from the New Mexico Photographic Survey project is the result of a shared labor of love. The efforts of these photographers and of J. B. Jackson reveal a sense of what we experience as New Mexico.

The New Mexico Photographic Survey project was directly supported by the time and efforts of the twelve photographers. Designed by the Museum of New Mexico, the project was funded by the National Endowment for the Arts with additional support from Sunwest Bank of Santa Fe. Special thanks to Luther Wilson, Richard Rudisill, Ed Ranney, Paul and Marcia Logsdon, Marc Simmons, Jill Z. Cooper, James Pahl, Marsha Jackson, and Theresa Arellano for their support and to the University of New Mexico Press for their persistence and encouragement. The New Mexico Photographic Survey, exhibited at the Museum of New Mexico in 1985, remains a part of the museum's permanent collection available to the public.

The Essential Landscape

Designed by Barbara Jellow
Composed by the
University of New Mexico Printing Plant
in Trump Medieval
Printed and bound in Japan by
DNP (America), Inc.